The ROI of Pharma 4.0

Dr. Jayant Joshi

Table of Contents

Part I: Introduction to Pharma 4.0 3

Introduction to Pharma 4.0 3
Overview of Pharma 4.0 and its significance in the pharmaceutical industry 4
Benefits of adopting Pharma 4.0 technologies 6

History and Evolution of Pharma 4.0 8
Historical context of Industry 4.0 and its adaptation in the pharmaceutical sector 10
Key milestones and early adopters 12

Current State of Pharma 4.0 Adoption 14
Current adoption rates and challenges faced by pharmaceutical companies. 16

Part II: Benefits of Pharma 4.0 21

Benefits of Pharma 4.0 21

Operational Efficiency and Productivity 23
How Pharma 4.0 enhances operational efficiency and productivity 23

Quality and Compliance 25
Role of Pharma 4.0 in improving product quality and regulatory compliance........ 25
Examples of real-time quality control and reduced quality losses 27

Innovation and Competitiveness 29
Impact of Pharma 4.0 on innovation and market competitiveness. 29

Part III: ROI of Pharma 4.0 33

ROI of Pharma 4.0 33

Calculating ROI in Pharma 4.0 35
Key metrics for measuring ROI: cost savings, efficiency gains, quality
improvements 37
Challenges in quantifying intangible benefits 39

Financial Benefits of Pharma 4.0 40
Cost Reduction Strategies: Automation, Predictive Maintenance, Reduced
Inventory Costs 42
Revenue growth opportunities: faster time-to-market, increased customer
satisfaction 44

Non-Financial Benefits of Pharma 4.0 46
Enhanced brand reputation, improved patient outcomes, increased employee
engagement 48
Sustainability and environmental benefits 50

Part IV: Implementing Pharma 4.0 55

Strategic Planning for Pharma 4.0 57
Steps for developing a strategic plan: assessing current state, setting objectives, creating a roadmap.. 59
Importance of stakeholder engagement and change management..................... 61

Technological Integration..63
Overview of key technologies: AI, IoT, blockchain, cloud computing................... 65
Best practices for integrating new technologies with existing systems................ 67

Change Management and Training 69
Strategies for managing cultural and operational changes 71
Training programs for enhancing digital literacy.. 73

Part V: Future Directions & Trends 77

Future Directions in Pharma 4.0..77

Future Trends in Pharma 4.0 79
Emerging technologies & innovations: GenAI, Digital Twins, Smart Manufacturing. 81
Future challenges and opportunities 82

Conclusion and Recommendations 84
Summary of key points and takeaways 86
Recommendations for pharmaceutical companies embarking on Pharma 4.0 journeys 88

Appendices 93

Glossary of Terms 93

ROI Calculator Template 95

Additional Resources 97

About the Author 101

Introduction to Pharma 4.0

Part I: Introduction to Pharma 4.0

Introduction to Pharma 4.0

Pharma 4.0 represents the integration of advanced digital technologies into the pharmaceutical industry, aligning with the principles of Industry 4.0. This transformation aims to enhance operational efficiency, product quality, and innovation by leveraging technologies such as Artificial Intelligence (AI), Internet of Things (IoT), Big Data Analytics, and cloud computing.

Key Concepts

1. **Digital Transformation:**
   - Integration of Technologies: Pharma 4.0 involves integrating AI, IoT, and big data analytics to transform manufacturing processes, drug development, and supply chain management.
   - Real-Time Monitoring: IoT devices enable real-time monitoring of critical parameters, ensuring consistent product quality and early detection of deviations.

2. **Applications:**
   - Drug Development: AI accelerates drug development by analysing large datasets and predicting drug efficacy.
   - Manufacturing: IoT and automation enhance operational efficiency and product quality.
   - Supply Chain Management: Real-time tracking and predictive analytics optimize inventory management and reduce supply chain risks.

3. **Benefits:**
   - Improved Efficiency: Streamlines processes, reducing costs and enhancing operational efficiency.
   - Enhanced Quality Control: Real-time monitoring ensures consistent product quality and early detection of deviations.
   - Innovation: Supports personalized medicine and accelerates innovation in drug development.
   - Regulatory Compliance: Ensures data integrity and compliance with regulatory standards.

Overview of Pharma 4.0 and its significance in the pharmaceutical industry

1. **Definition and Purpose:**

   o Pharma 4.0 Concept: A comprehensive framework that integrates digital technologies to transform pharmaceutical manufacturing, drug development, and digital supply chain management.

   o It is an extension of Industry 4.0, tailored to address the unique challenges of the pharmaceutical sector.

   o Benefits: Enhances operational efficiency, improves product quality, better operational and business excellence, and supports personalized medicine by enabling precise control over manufacturing processes and leveraging data insights.

2. **Key Technologies:**

   o AI and Machine Learning: Used for predictive analytics, process optimization, and personalized medicine development.

   o IoT and Sensors: Enable real-time monitoring and automation in pharma smart manufacturing processes.

   o Big Data Analytics: Processes large datasets to extract insights that improve pharma manufacturing efficiency and better product quality.

   o Cloud Computing: Provides scalable data management and collaboration across different departments.

3. **Applications:**

   o Drug Development: AI accelerates drug development by analyzing large datasets and predicting drug efficacy.

   o Manufacturing: IoT and process automation enhance operational efficiency and consistent product quality.

   o Digital Supply Chain Management: Real-time tracking and predictive analytics optimize real-time inventory management and reduce supply chain management risks.

4. **Benefits:**
   o Improved Manufacturing Efficiency: Streamlines processes, reducing operational costs and enhancing operational efficiency.
   o Enhanced Quality Control: Real-time monitoring ensures consistent product quality and early detection of deviations.
   o Innovation: Supports personalized medicine and accelerates innovation in drug development.
   o Regulatory Compliance: Ensures data integrity and compliance with regulatory standards.

Significance in the Pharmaceutical Industry

Pharma 4.0 is significant because it transforms traditional manufacturing processes into more efficient, data-driven operations. This shift enables pharmaceutical companies to:

- Improve Patient Outcomes and centricity: By developing personalized treatments and ensuring consistent product quality.

- Enhance Competitiveness: Through accelerated innovation and reduced time-to-market for new drugs and treatments.

- Meet Regulatory Requirements: By maintaining data integrity and compliance with evolving regulatory compliance standards.

Requirements

- Data Quality Management: Ensuring high-quality data is crucial for accurate insights and informed decision-making.

- Technological Integration: Leveraging advanced emerging technologies like AI and IoT to analyse complex datasets.

- Regulatory Frameworks: Understanding and adhering to evolving regulatory standards to maintain compliance.

By embracing Pharma 4.0, pharmaceutical companies can transform their manufacturing operations, enhance product quality, and improve patient care while maintaining regulatory compliance.

Benefits of adopting Pharma 4.0 technologies

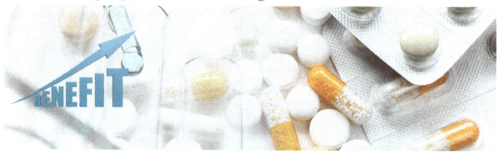

Adopting Pharma 4.0 technologies offers several benefits to the pharmaceutical industry, transforming operations and enhancing patient outcomes. Here are some of the key advantages:

1. **Improved Efficiency and Productivity:**

   o Real-Time Monitoring: Enables real-time monitoring of smart manufacturing processes, allowing for quick identification and resolution of issues, reducing downtime and enhancing production efficiency.

   o Predictive Maintenance: Predictive analytics minimize unplanned equipment downtime, ensuring continuous production and optimizing resource utilization.

   o Lean Manufacturing Practices: Digital tools support lean principles by minimizing waste and optimizing workflows, enhancing manufacturing operational efficiency.

2. **Enhanced Quality Control:**

   o Early Detection of Quality Issues: Advanced analytics and machine learning identify quality deviations early in the manufacturing process, ensuring consistent product quality and reducing the risk of recalls.

   o Data Integrity: Maintains data integrity through digital records and automated workflows, supporting regulatory compliance.

3. **Personalized Medicine:**

   o Tailored Treatments: Enables the development of personalized treatments by analyzing large-scale medical records and leveraging data insights to tailor therapies to individual patient needs.

   o Improved Patient Outcomes: Personalized medicine enhances treatment efficacy and reduces adverse reactions, improving patient outcomes and satisfaction.

4. **Digital Supply Chain Optimization:**

   o Real-Time Tracking: Technologies like IoT and blockchain enable real-time monitoring of the digital supply chain, enhancing transparency and traceability.

   o Inventory Management: Predictive analytics optimize inventory levels, reducing stockouts and overstocking.

5. **Increased Innovation and Competitiveness:**

   o   Accelerated Drug Development: AI and machine learning accelerate drug development, enabling faster time-to-market for new product and treatments.

   o   Adaptability to Market Changes: Enhances the industry's ability to respond to changing market demands and customer needs for Demand Forecasting.

6. **Simplified Compliance and Regulatory Oversight:**

   o   Digital Records: Provides transparent and reliable digital records of the entire drug product lifecycle, simplifying compliance and regulatory oversight.

   o   Proactive Risk Management: Facilitates a proactive and risk-based approach to compliance, enhancing collaboration with regulatory bodies.

By embracing Pharma 4.0 technologies, pharmaceutical companies can enhance operational efficiency, improve product quality, and drive innovation while maintaining regulatory compliance.

History and Evolution of Pharma 4.0

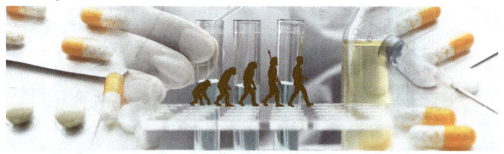

The history and evolution of Pharma 4.0 are deeply rooted in the broader context of Industry 4.0, which began in 2011 in Germany as part of a government initiative to enhance manufacturing efficiency through digital technologies like Cloud, AI, IoT, and robotics.

1. **Origins of Industry 4.0:**

   o 2011: The concept of Industry 4.0 was first introduced in Germany as part of a government initiative to enhance manufacturing efficiency through digital technologies.

   o Pharma 4.0 Emergence: Although the term Pharma 4.0 was mentioned in 2011, it gained significant traction later as an extension of Industry 4.0 principles to the pharmaceutical sector.

2. **Pharma 4.0 Development:**

   o 2017: The term Pharma 4.0 was formally recognized by the International Society for Pharmaceutical Engineering (ISPE) to adapt Industry 4.0 principles to the pharmaceutical industry. This marked a significant step towards integrating advanced technologies into drug development and manufacturing processes.

   o White Paper Publication: In 2017, a white paper titled "Pharma 4.0: A Roadmap for Digital Pharmaceutical Manufacturing" was published by German researchers and industry experts, outlining a roadmap for digital transformation in pharmaceutical manufacturing.

3. **Evolution and Adoption:**

   o Early Adoption: Initially, Pharma 4.0 focused on leveraging technologies to improve operational efficiency and product quality. It involved the integration of Cloud, AI, IoT, and big data analytics to streamline manufacturing processes and enhance digital supply chain management.

   o Current Developments: Today, Pharma 4.0 is recognized for its potential to accelerate drug development, improve regulatory compliance, and enable personalized medicine through advanced data analysis and automation with Digital Transformation.

4. Key Milestones:

- o ISPE's Role: ISPE has played a crucial role in providing guidance and best practices for Pharma 4.0 implementation, helping to harmonize the adoption of digital technologies across the industry.

- o Conferences and Workshops: Regular conferences and workshops, such as those organized by ISPE, have facilitated knowledge sharing and collaboration among stakeholders, further advancing the adoption of Pharma 4.0 technologies.

5. Future Directions:

- o Increased Adoption: As more companies adopt Pharma 4.0, there is a growing focus on addressing regulatory challenges and ensuring data security while enhancing patient outcomes.

- o Technological Advancements: The integration of emerging technologies like blockchain and advanced AI models is expected to further transform the pharma industry, enabling more efficient and personalized healthcare solutions.

By understanding this evolution, pharmaceutical companies can better navigate the transition to Pharma 4.0 and leverage its potential to drive innovation and efficiency in drug development and manufacturing.

Assume

- Data Quality Management: Ensuring high-quality data is crucial for accurate insights and informed decision-making.

- Technological Integration: Leveraging advanced technologies like AI and IoT to analyze complex datasets.

- Regulatory Frameworks: Understanding and adhering to evolving regulatory standards to maintain compliance.

Historical context of Industry 4.0 and its adaptation in the pharmaceutical sector

Industry 4.0, also known as the fourth industrial revolution, was first introduced in Germany in 2011. It emphasizes the integration of advanced digital technologies such as Cloud, Artificial Intelligence (AI), Internet of Things (IoT), and Big Data Analytics into manufacturing processes. This concept has been adapted in various sectors, including the pharmaceutical industry, as Pharma 4.0.

1. **Introduction of Industry 4.0:**

   o 2011: Industry 4.0 was first introduced at Hannover MESSE in Germany, focusing on integrating information and communication technology into industrial production.

   o German Government Initiative: The German government supported this initiative through the "High-Tech Strategy 2020" action plan in 2012, which encouraged the adoption of Industry 4.0 principles across industries.

2. **Adaptation in Pharmaceuticals:**

   o Pharma 4.0 Emergence: The term Pharma 4.0 emerged as an extension of Industry 4.0, specifically tailored for the pharmaceutical sector. It aims to leverage digital technologies to enhance operational efficiency, product quality, and innovation in drug development and manufacturing.

   o ISPE's Role: The International Society for Pharmaceutical Engineering (ISPE) has played a crucial role in developing guidelines and roadmaps for implementing Pharma 4.0, ensuring alignment with regulatory standards and best practices.

3. **Key Technologies and Applications:**

   o AI and IoT: Used for predictive analytics, real-time monitoring, and automation in manufacturing processes.

   o Big Data Analytics: Processes large datasets to extract insights that improve manufacturing operation efficiency and product quality.

   o Cloud Computing: Provides scalable data management and collaboration across different departments.

4. **Benefits and Challenges:**

   o Benefits: Enhances operational efficiency, improves product quality, and supports personalized medicine.

   o Challenges: Includes managing cultural resistance, ensuring regulatory compliance, and integrating new technologies with existing systems.

By adapting Industry 4.0 principles, the pharmaceutical sector can transform its operations, enhance patient outcomes, and maintain competitiveness in a rapidly evolving industry landscape.

Prerequisites

- Data Quality Management: Ensuring high-quality data is crucial for accurate insights and informed decision-making.

- Technological Integration: Leveraging advanced technologies like Cloud, AI and IoT to analyse complex datasets.

- Regulatory Frameworks: Understanding and adhering to evolving regulatory standards to maintain compliance.

Key milestones and early adopters

1. **Introduction of Industry 4.0 (2011):**

   o German Government Initiative: Industry 4.0 was first introduced in Germany as part of a government initiative to enhance manufacturing efficiency through digital technologies.

   o Extension to Pharmaceuticals: The concept later extended to the pharmaceutical sector as Pharma 4.0.

2. **Emergence of Pharma 4.0 (2017):**

   o ISPE's Role: The International Society for Pharmaceutical Engineering (ISPE) formally introduced Pharma 4.0 in 2017, adapting Industry 4.0 principles to the pharmaceutical sector.

   o White Paper Publication: A white paper titled "Pharma 4.0: A Roadmap for Digital Pharmaceutical Manufacturing" was published, outlining a roadmap for digital transformation in pharmaceutical manufacturing.

3. **Recent Developments:**

   o Market Growth: The Pharma 4.0 market is projected to grow significantly, with estimates suggesting it will reach over $67.7 billion by 2033, driven by the adoption of emerging technologies like AI, IoT, and cloud computing.

   o Technological Advancements: Recent trends include the use of digital twins, predictive maintenance, and AI-driven decision-making to optimize pharma manufacturing processes and reduce downtime.

Early Adopters

1. **Big Pharma Companies:**

   o A large pharma company has seen significant improvements in operational efficiency and innovation through Pharma 4.0 investments, including a 50% reduction in unplanned downtime.

   o A pharma company has successfully integrated digital technologies to enhance operational efficiency and innovation, improving drug development processes and optimizing manufacturing operations.

2. Technology Providers:

- o Siemens Healthcare, GE Healthcare, IBM, Microsoft, Amazon Web Services, and Oracle: These companies are collaborating with pharmaceutical giants to create cutting-edge AI and cloud-based solutions for Pharma 4.0.

These early adopters have demonstrated the potential of Pharma 4.0 to transform the pharmaceutical industry by enhancing efficiency, quality, and innovation.

Current State of Pharma 4.0 Adoption

The current state of Pharma 4.0 adoption reflects a transformative phase in the pharmaceutical industry, driven by advancements in digital technologies, evolving regulations, and increasing global demand for innovative solutions. Here's an overview of the current adoption state:

1. **Market Growth and Trends:**
   - Market Size: The Pharma 4.0 market is valued at approximately USD 14.05 billion in 2023 and is projected to reach USD 61 billion by 2032 at a CAGR of 17.8%.
   - Emerging Trends: Key trends include the integration of AI, IoT, and blockchain to enhance operational efficiency, improve product quality, and support personalized medicine.

2. **Technological Integration:**
   - AI and Machine Learning: AI and ML are being increasingly used for drug development, predictive analytics, and manufacturing process optimization, accelerating innovation and reducing development timelines.
   - IoT and Automation: IoT devices and automation technologies are transforming manufacturing processes by enabling real-time monitoring and reducing downtime.

3. **Regulatory Environment:**
   - Regulatory Support: Regulatory bodies are increasingly supportive of digital transformation, with efforts to harmonize standards and encourage the adoption of advanced manufacturing technologies.
   - Challenges: Despite technology progress, regulatory uncertainties and the need for international convergence remain challenges for widespread adoption.

4. **Industry Adoption:**
   - Early Adopters: Major pharmaceutical companies are leading the way in adopting Pharma 4.0 technologies, demonstrating significant improvements in operational efficiency and innovation.
   - Global Expansion: The adoption of Pharma 4.0 is expanding globally, with North America playing a significant role due to its robust healthcare infrastructure and technological advancements.

5. **Challenges and Opportunities:**

   o   Challenges: Common challenges include managing cultural resistance, ensuring regulatory compliance, and addressing data privacy and security concerns.

   o   Opportunities: Offers opportunities for accelerated innovation, improved efficiency, and enhanced patient outcomes, ultimately driving business success and competitiveness in the pharmaceutical industry.

By embracing Pharma 4.0, pharmaceutical companies can transform their operations, enhance product quality, and improve patient care while maintaining regulatory compliance.

Factors to consider

- Data Quality Management: Ensuring high-quality data is crucial for accurate insights and informed decision-making.

- Technological Integration: Leveraging advanced technologies like Cloud, AI and IoT to analyze complex datasets.

- Regulatory Frameworks: Understanding and adhering to evolving regulatory standards to maintain compliance.

Current adoption rates and challenges faced by pharmaceutical companies.

The current adoption rates of Pharma 4.0 technologies in the pharmaceutical industry are still relatively low, with only about 1% to 3% of companies qualifying as fully integrated Pharma 4.0 facilities. However, there is a growing trend towards digital transformation, with approximately 55% of pharma companies expected to start adoption of digital technologies by 2025.

Current Adoption Rates

- Digital Transformation: By 2025, about 55% of pharmaceutical companies are expected to start the adoption of digital technologies, reflecting a significant shift from traditional practices.

- Pharma 4.0 Adoption: Despite the potential benefits, only a small percentage of pharmaceutical companies have fully implemented Pharma 4.0 technologies, highlighting a gap in widespread adoption.

Challenges Faced by Pharmaceutical Companies

1. **Regulatory Compliance:**
   - Stringent Regulations: Ensuring that new emerging technologies meet regulatory standards is a significant challenge. Regulatory frameworks often lag behind technological advancements, creating uncertainty for manufacturers.
   - Global Variability: Different regulatory requirements across countries complicate compliance efforts.

2. **Data Privacy and Security:**
   - Sensitive Data Management: The use of Cloud, AI, IoT, and big data analytics generates vast amounts of sensitive data, requiring robust cyber security measures to protect against cyber threats and ensure data integrity.
   - Compliance with Data Regulations: Adhering to data protection laws like GDPR adds complexity to data management.

3. **Integration of Legacy Systems:**
   - Technical Challenges: Integrating new digital technologies with existing legacy systems can be complex and costly.
   - System Compatibility: Ensuring compatibility between old and new systems is crucial for seamless data sharing operations.

4. **Talent Acquisition and Retention:**

   o   Skill Gaps: Pharma 4.0 requires specialized skills in areas like Cloud, AI, machine learning, and data analytics, which can be difficult to find and retain.

   o   Training and Development: Continuous training is necessary to keep employees up-to-date with evolving emerging technologies.

5. **High Investment Costs:**

   o   Initial Investment: Implementing Pharma 4.0 technologies requires significant upfront investment in infrastructure, software, and talent.

   o   ROI Uncertainty: The return on investment can be uncertain, especially for smaller companies with limited resources.

By addressing these challenges proactively, pharmaceutical companies can navigate the complexities of Pharma 4.0 and leverage its potential to drive innovation and efficiency.

Factors to consider

- Data Quality Management: Ensuring high-quality data is crucial for accurate insights and informed decision-making.

- Technological Integration: Leveraging advanced technologies like AI and IoT to analyze complex datasets.

- Regulatory Frameworks: Understanding and adhering to evolving regulatory standards to maintain compliance.

Benefits of Pharma 4.0

Part II: Benefits of Pharma 4.0

Benefits of Pharma 4.0

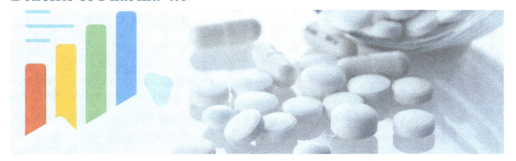

Here's an overview of the benefits of Pharma 4.0, highlighting how it transforms the pharmaceutical industry:

1. **Improved Manufacturing Efficiency:**

   o Real-Time Monitoring: Enables real-time monitoring of manufacturing processes, allowing for quick identification and resolution of issues, reducing downtime and enhancing production efficiency.

   o Predictive Maintenance: Predictive analytics minimize unplanned equipment downtime, ensuring continuous production and optimizing resource utilization.

2. **Enhanced Quality Control:**

   o Early Detection of Quality Issues: Advanced analytics and machine learning identify quality deviations early in the manufacturing process, ensuring consistent product quality and reducing defects.

   o Data Integrity: Maintains data integrity through digital records and automated workflows, supporting regulatory compliance.

3. **Personalized Medicine:**

   o Tailored Treatments: Enables the development of personalized treatments by analysing large-scale medical records and leveraging data insights to tailor therapies to individual patient needs.

   o Improved Patient Outcomes: Personalized medicine enhances treatment efficacy and reduces adverse reactions, improving patient outcomes.

4. **Improved Digital Supply Chain Management:**

   o Real-Time Product Batch Tracking: Technologies like IoT and blockchain enable real-time monitoring of the digital supply chain, enhancing transparency and traceability.

   o Inventory Management: Predictive analytics optimize inventory levels, reducing stockouts and overstocking.

21

5. **Increased Patient Safety:**

   o   Consistent Quality: Ensures consistent product quality, reducing the risk of errors and improving patient safety.

   o   Personalized Treatments: Enables more effective treatments tailored to individual patient needs, enhancing patient outcomes.

6. **Faster Time to Market:**

   o   Accelerated Drug Development: Uses advanced analytics and machine learning to accelerate drug development, reducing time-to-market for new treatments.

   o   Efficient Clinical Trials: Optimizes clinical trial processes through real-time data analysis and predictive modelling.

7. **Innovation and Competitiveness:**

   o   Innovation: Supports innovation by enabling flexible manufacturing processes and personalized medicine.

   o   Competitive Advantage: Enhances competitiveness by improving operational efficiency and reducing costs.

By leveraging these benefits, pharmaceutical companies can transform their operations, enhance product quality, and improve patient care while maintaining regulatory compliance.

Operational Efficiency and Productivity

How Pharma 4.0 enhances operational efficiency and productivity

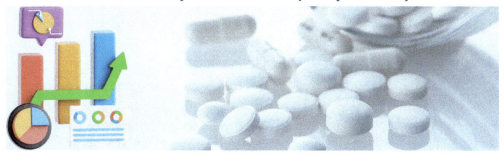

Pharma 4.0 enhances operational efficiency and productivity in the pharmaceutical industry by leveraging advanced digital technologies such as Artificial Intelligence (AI), Internet of Things (IoT), Big Data Analytics, and cloud computing. Here's how these technologies contribute to operational efficiency and productivity:

1. **Real-Time Monitoring and Control:**

   o IoT Sensors: IoT devices enable real-time data monitoring of critical parameters in manufacturing processes, allowing for swift identification and resolution of issues, reducing downtime and enhancing production efficiency.

   o Predictive Maintenance: Predictive analytics from IoT data help predict equipment failures, minimizing unplanned downtime and ensuring continuous production.

2. **Automation and Robotics:**

   o Streamlined Processes: Robotics and automation streamline manufacturing processes, reducing manual errors and improving efficiency by minimizing human intervention.

   o Optimized Workflows: Automated workflows optimize resource allocation and reduce waste, enhancing overall equipment effectiveness (OEE).

3. **Data-Driven Decision Making:**

   o Big Data Analytics: Advanced analytics process large datasets to extract insights that optimize smart manufacturing processes, improve quality control, and enhance digital supply chain management.

   o AI-Driven Insights: AI algorithms analyze data to identify trends and patterns, enabling informed decisions that improve manufacturing operational efficiency and product quality.

4. **Supply Chain Optimization:**

   o Real-Time Tracking: Technologies like blockchain and IoT enable real-time tracking of products, ensuring quality and authenticity throughout the digital supply chain.

   o Inventory Management: Predictive analytics optimize inventory management, minimizing stockouts and overstocking.

5. Digitalization and Integration:

- o Seamless Data Exchange: Digital platforms facilitate real-time data exchange across departments, enhancing collaboration and reducing manual data entry errors.

- o Lean Manufacturing Practices: Pharma 4.0 aligns with lean principles to minimize waste and optimize workflows, further improving efficiency.

Benefits of Enhanced Operational Efficiency

- Cost Savings: Enhanced efficiency reduces operational costs by minimizing waste and optimizing resource allocation.

- Increased Productivity: Improved OEE (Overall Equipment Effectiveness) and reduced downtime lead to higher production volumes and faster time-to-market for new products.

- Enhanced Quality: Real-time monitoring ensures consistent product quality, reducing the risk of deviations and recalls.

- Competitive Advantage: Supports competitiveness by enabling pharmaceutical companies to respond more quickly to market demands and customer needs.

By leveraging these emerging technologies, pharmaceutical companies can enhance operational efficiency, improve productivity, and drive innovation while maintaining regulatory compliance.

Quality and Compliance

Role of Pharma 4.0 in improving product quality and regulatory compliance.

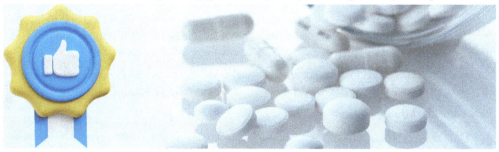

Pharma 4.0 plays a crucial role in improving product quality and regulatory compliance in the pharmaceutical industry. Here's how it achieves these goals:

Role of Pharma 4.0 in Improving Product Quality

1. **Real-Time Monitoring and Control:**

   o IoT Sensors: IoT devices enable real-time monitoring of critical parameters in manufacturing processes, allowing for early detection of quality issues and prompt corrective actions.

   o Predictive Analytics: AI-driven predictive analytics help identify potential quality risks early in the manufacturing process, ensuring consistent product quality.

2. **Enhanced Quality Control:**

   o Data Integrity: Pharma 4.0 technologies maintain data integrity through digital records and automated workflows, supporting regulatory compliance with standards like 21 CFR Part 11.

   o Quality-by-Design (QbD): QbD processes focus on controlling product quality within specific parameters, ensuring that products meet quality standards from the outset.

3. **Personalized Medicine:**

   o Tailored Treatments: Enables the development of personalized treatments by analysing large-scale medical records and leveraging data insights to tailor therapies to individual patient needs.

Role of Pharma 4.0 in Improving Regulatory Compliance

1. **Data Transparency and Integrity:**

   o Blockchain Technology: Blockchain ensures secure and transparent data management, aligning with evolving regulatory requirements and maintaining compliance throughout the product lifecycle.

   o Electronic Documentation: Intelligent compliance systems driven by blockchain, AI, and electronic documentation ensure compliance on an instant basis.

2. **Regulatory Oversight:**

   o   Proactive Compliance Approach: Pharma 4.0 enables a proactive and risk-based approach to compliance, enhancing collaboration with regulators and auditors.

   o   Compliance with Evolving Regulations: Technologies like Cloud, AI and blockchain help pharmaceutical companies comply with increasingly stringent regulatory requirements by improving data quality, accuracy, and transparency.

By leveraging these technologies, pharmaceutical companies can enhance product quality, improve regulatory compliance, and maintain a robust quality culture.

Key Considerations

- Data Quality Management: Ensuring high-quality data is crucial for accurate insights and informed decision-making.

- Technological Integration: Leveraging advanced technologies like AI and IoT to analyse complex datasets.

- Regulatory Frameworks: Understanding and adhering to evolving regulatory standards to maintain compliance.

Examples of real-time quality control and reduced quality losses

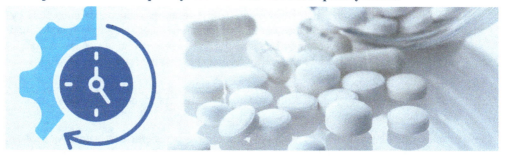

Here are some examples of real-time quality control and reduced quality losses achieved through Pharma 4.0 technologies:

1. **McKinsey's Report on Quality Control:**

   o Real-Time Monitoring: McKinsey highlights that real-time monitoring and automation can reduce quality control costs by more than 50% and improve productivity by 50 to 100% in well-performing labs. This is achieved through the use of advanced analytics and automation, which enable faster and more effective problem resolution.

   o Deviation Reduction: Digitization and automation have resulted in a more than 65% reduction in overall deviations and over 90% faster closure times, significantly improving quality control efficiency.

2. **IoT-Enabled Sensors for Quality Control:**

   o Real-Time Data Collection: IoT sensors allow for real-time monitoring of critical production variables, ensuring that pharmaceutical products meet the highest standards. This technology detects deviations early, preventing quality issues and reducing the risk of costly recalls.

   o Predictive Maintenance: By analyzing data from machinery, manufacturers can foresee potential failures before they disrupt production, minimizing equipment downtime and enhancing operational efficiency.

3. **Real-Time Release Testing (RTRT):**

   o Efficient Quality Assessment: RTRT is an advanced approach that evaluates product quality in real-time during manufacturing, enabling faster release of medications and reducing the need for post-production testing. This method improves process flexibility and adaptability by consistently quantifying inter- and intra-batch variability.

   o Case Studies: Large Global Pharma Companies have successfully implemented RTRT, achieving regulatory approval and improving efficiency in their manufacturing processes.

4. Paperless Quality Solutions:

- o Digital Logbooks and Batch Records: Paperless solutions reduce data entry time by up to 85%, enhance compliance with documentation + data integrity principles, and minimize the risk of receiving FDA warning letters. These digital systems ensure that all data is stored in an audit-ready format, simplifying regulatory audits.

- o Improved Compliance: By automating data recording and enforcing mandatory data entry, these systems reduce errors and ensure that all production records are accurate and traceable.

These examples demonstrate how Pharma 4.0 technologies can significantly enhance real-time quality control, reduce quality losses, and improve regulatory compliance in the pharmaceutical industry.

Innovation and Competitiveness

Impact of Pharma 4.0 on innovation and market competitiveness.

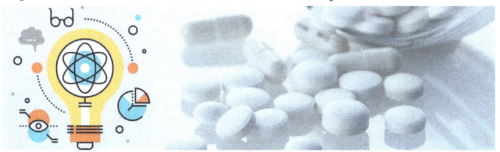

Pharma 4.0 has a profound impact on innovation and market competitiveness in the pharmaceutical industry. Here's how it enhances both:

1. **Accelerated Drug Development:**

   o   AI and Machine Learning: AI and ML accelerate drug discovery by analysing large datasets, predicting drug efficacy, and optimizing lead compounds. This reduces the time and cost associated with bringing new drugs to market.

   o   Data-Driven Insights: Big data analytics provide insights that help identify new therapeutic targets and optimize clinical trial designs, enhancing innovation in drug development.

2. **Personalized Medicine:**

   o   Tailored Treatments: Pharma 4.0 enables the development of personalized treatments by leveraging data insights to tailor therapies to individual patient needs. This approach improves treatment efficacy and reduces adverse reactions.

3. **Smart Manufacturing and Flexibility:**

   o   Modular Production Facilities: Modular facilities enabled by Pharma 4.0 allow for flexible production processes, enabling companies to respond quickly to changing market demands and customer needs.

   o   Digital Twins: Digital twins simulate manufacturing processes, allowing for real-time analytics and optimization without disrupting actual production. This enhances operational flexibility and reduces downtime.

Impact of Pharma 4.0 on Market Competitiveness

1. **Competitive Advantage:**

   o   Innovation Leadership: Companies that adopt Pharma 4.0 technologies can gain a competitive edge by innovating faster and more efficiently than competitors.

   o   Regulatory Compliance Simplification: Pharma 4.0 simplifies compliance processes through process automation and data integrity, reducing regulatory risks and enhancing competitiveness.

2. **Operational Efficiency and Cost Reduction:**
   o Smart Manufacturing: The adoption of smart manufacturing technologies, including robotics and IoT-enabled devices, automates complex production processes, improves operational efficiency, and reduces production costs.
   o Predictive Analytics: Predictive analytics enable faster, more accurate decision-making, allowing pharmaceutical companies to bring drugs to market more efficiently.

3. **Digital Supply Chain Optimization:**
   o Real-Time Tracking and Traceability: Technologies like Cloud, IoT and blockchain enhance supply chain transparency and traceability, reducing risks and ensuring product authenticity.
   o Predictive Analytics: Predictive analytics optimize inventory management and logistics, improving supply chain efficiency and reducing costs.

By leveraging these innovations, pharmaceutical companies can enhance their competitiveness, drive business success, and improve patient outcomes.

Key Considerations

- Data Quality Management: Ensuring high-quality data is crucial for accurate insights and informed decision-making.

- Technological Integration: Leveraging advanced technologies like AI and IoT to analyse complex datasets.

- Regulatory Frameworks: Understanding and adhering to evolving regulatory standards to maintain compliance.

Challenges and Opportunities

- Challenges: Common challenges include managing cultural resistance, ensuring regulatory compliance, and integrating new technologies with existing systems.

- Opportunities: Offers opportunities for accelerated innovation, improved efficiency, and enhanced patient outcomes, ultimately driving business success and competitiveness in the pharmaceutical industry.

ROI of Pharma 4.0

Part III: ROI of Pharma 4.0

ROI of Pharma 4.0

Here's an overview of the Return on Investment (ROI) of Pharma 4.0, highlighting how it enhances operational efficiency, innovation, and competitiveness in the pharmaceutical industry:

1. **Operational Efficiency and Cost Savings:**

   o OEE (Overall Equipment Effectiveness) Improvement: Pharma 4.0 technologies can significantly improve Overall Equipment Effectiveness (OEE) by reducing downtime and enhancing performance. For instance, improving OEE from 37% to 70% can increase annual returns by $15M to $21M for a typical pharma factory.

   o Cost Reduction: Automation and advanced analytics reduce operational costs by minimizing waste, predicting demand more accurately, and optimizing resource allocation.

2. **Innovation and Time-to-Market:**

   o Accelerated Drug Development: AI and data analytics accelerate the drug development process, enabling faster time-to-market for new treatments and improving competitiveness.

   o Personalized Medicine: Enables the development of personalized treatments, enhancing patient outcomes and creating new revenue streams.

3. **Quality Improvements and Regulatory Compliance:**

   o Enhanced Quality Control: Real-time monitoring and automated systems ensure higher quality standards and early identification of potential issues, reducing quality losses and improving regulatory compliance.

   o Regulatory Compliance: Simplifies compliance processes through automation and data integrity, reducing regulatory risks and associated costs.

4. **Digital Supply Chain Optimization:**

   o Real-Time Tracking and Traceability: Technologies like Cloud, IoT and blockchain enhance supply chain transparency and traceability, reducing risks and ensuring product authenticity.

   o Predictive Analytics: Optimize inventory management and logistics, improving supply chain efficiency and reducing costs.

5. **Intangible Benefits:**

   o Enhanced Brand Reputation: Digital transformation can improve brand reputation and customer trust through better quality control and patient outcomes.

   o Increased Innovation and Agility: Enables pharmaceutical companies to respond more quickly to market changes and disruptions, enhancing their competitive edge.

Challenges in Measuring ROI (Return On Investment)

- Data Quality and Integration: Accurate data is essential for calculating ROI, but integrating data from different systems can be complex.

- Long-Term Perspective: Many benefits of Pharma 4.0, such as improved decision-making and competitive advantage, may take time to materialize.

- Intangible Benefits: Quantifying intangible benefits like enhanced brand reputation and customer satisfaction can be challenging.

Key Considerations

- Data Quality Management: Ensuring high-quality data is crucial for accurate ROI calculations and informed decision-making.

- Technological Integration: Leveraging advanced technologies like AI and IoT to analyze complex datasets and improve operational efficiency.

- Regulatory Frameworks: Understanding and adhering to evolving regulatory standards to maintain compliance and ensure ROI sustainability.

Calculating ROI in Pharma 4.0

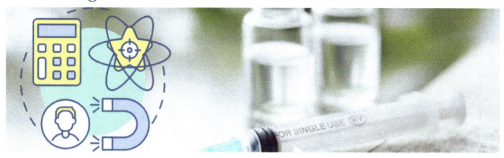

Calculating the Return on Investment (ROI) in Pharma 4.0 involves assessing various financial and non-financial metrics to evaluate the effectiveness of digital transformation initiatives. Here's a structured approach to calculating ROI in Pharma 4.0:

1. **Identify Key Metrics:**

   o Cost Savings: Reduced operational costs through automation and process optimization.

   o Efficiency Gains: Improved productivity and throughput.

   o Quality Improvements: Reduced error rates and improved product quality.

   o Revenue Growth: Faster time-to-market for new products and increased customer satisfaction.

2. **Quantify Benefits:**

   o Financial Benefits: Calculate cost savings, increased revenue, and improved profitability.

   o Intangible Benefits: Assess improvements in brand reputation, employee morale, and innovation agility.

3. **Calculate ROI:**

   o ROI Formula: ROI = (Net Gain from Investment / Cost of Investment) x 100.

   o Example: If a Pharma 4.0 initiative costs $1 million and results in a net gain of $1.5 million, the ROI is 50%.

4. **Use ROI Calculators:**

   o Digital Factory ROI Calculator: Various Tools are available in market for ROI calculator help estimate returns by considering OEE improvements and productivity gains.

5. **Challenges in ROI Calculation:**

  o Long-Term vs. Short-Term Gains: Some benefits may take time to materialize.

  o Intangible Benefits: Difficult to quantify benefits like enhanced brand reputation and employee satisfaction.

  o Data Integration: Complexities in gathering and analyzing data from disparate systems.

Assumptions

- Data Quality Management: Ensuring high-quality data is crucial for accurate ROI calculations and informed decision-making.

- Technological Integration: Leveraging advanced technologies like AI and IoT to analyze complex datasets.

- Regulatory Frameworks: Understanding and adhering to evolving regulatory standards to maintain compliance.

Ready for Challenges and Opportunities

- Challenges: Common challenges include managing cultural resistance, ensuring regulatory compliance, and integrating new technologies with existing systems.

- Opportunities: Offers opportunities for accelerated innovation, improved efficiency, and enhanced patient outcomes, ultimately driving business success and competitiveness in the pharmaceutical industry.

Key metrics for measuring ROI: cost savings, efficiency gains, quality improvements

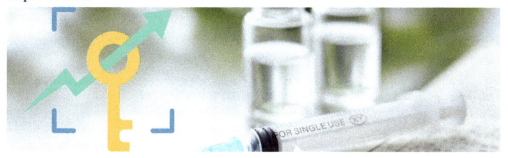

Measuring the Return on Investment (ROI) in Pharma 4.0 involves tracking several key metrics that reflect cost savings, efficiency gains, and quality improvements. Here's an overview of these metrics:

1. **Cost Savings:**

   o Operational Cost Reduction: Automation and process optimization reduce operational costs by minimizing waste and improving resource allocation.

   o Inventory Management: Predictive analytics optimize inventory levels, reducing inventory carrying costs and minimizing stockouts.

   o Reduced Recall Costs: Improved quality control reduces the risk of product recalls, saving costs associated with recalls and regulatory penalties.

2. **Efficiency Gains:**

   o Improved Productivity: Enhanced OEE (Overall Equipment Effectiveness) and reduced downtime increase production volumes and efficiency.

   o Streamlined Processes: Digitalization simplifies workflows, reducing cycle times and improving asset utilization.

   o Faster Time-to-Market: Accelerated drug development and approval processes enable faster market entry for new products.

3. **Quality Improvements:**

   o Reduced Error Rates: Real-time monitoring and automation minimize manual errors, improving product quality and consistency.

   o Enhanced Compliance: Improved data integrity and regulatory compliance reduce the risk of deviations and regulatory actions.

   o Patient Safety: Personalized medicine and targeted therapies enhance patient outcomes by tailoring treatments to individual needs.

Key Considerations

- Data Quality Management: Ensuring high-quality data is crucial for accurate ROI calculations and informed decision-making.

- Technological Integration: Leveraging advanced technologies like AI and IoT to analyse complex datasets.

- Regulatory Frameworks: Understanding and adhering to evolving regulatory standards to maintain compliance.

Challenges and Opportunities

- Challenges: Common challenges include managing cultural resistance, ensuring regulatory compliance, and integrating new technologies with existing systems.

- Opportunities: Offers opportunities for accelerated innovation, improved efficiency, and enhanced patient outcomes, ultimately driving business success and competitiveness in the pharmaceutical industry.

Challenges in quantifying intangible benefits

Quantifying intangible benefits in the context of Pharma 4.0 can be challenging due to their non-financial nature and the difficulty in assigning a monetary value. Here are some of the challenges and strategies for addressing them:

1. **Nature of Intangible Benefits:**

   o Definition: Intangible benefits are those that cannot be easily measured or quantified in financial terms, such as enhanced brand reputation, improved employee morale, and increased innovation capacity.

   o Characteristics. These benefits often relate to strategic advantages, such as better decision-making, improved customer satisfaction, and enhanced competitiveness.

2. **Measurement Challenges:**

   o Lack of Direct Metrics: There are no direct metrics to quantify intangible benefits, making it difficult to assess their impact on the bottom line.

   o Subjective Evaluation: Intangible benefits often require subjective evaluation, which can vary depending on individual perspectives and organizational goals.

3. **Quantification Strategies:**

   o Relative Quantification: Compare intangible benefits to tangible ones or use relative metrics to estimate their value. For example, comparing the impact of improved brand reputation on customer loyalty versus direct financial gains.

   o Scenario Analysis: Use scenario analysis to estimate the potential outcomes of intangible benefits. This involves assessing the likelihood and potential impact of these benefits on business operations.

   o Surveys and Feedback: Conduct surveys among stakeholders, such as employees or customers, to gather feedback on perceived benefits and their impact on organizational performance.

4. **Benefits Realization Plan:**

   o Implementation: Develop a benefits realization plan to outline activities necessary for achieving planned benefits. This plan should include timelines, tools, and resources needed to ensure that benefits are fully realized over time.

   o Oversight: Assign oversight to ensure that intangible benefits are monitored and evaluated regularly, adjusting strategies as needed to maximize their impact.

Financial Benefits of Pharma 4.0

The financial benefits of Pharma 4.0 are substantial, encompassing cost savings, efficiency gains, and revenue growth opportunities. Here's an overview of these benefits:

1. **Cost Savings:**

   o   Operational Efficiency: Automation and process optimization reduce operational costs by minimizing waste and improving resource allocation.

   o   Inventory Management: Predictive analytics optimize inventory levels, reducing inventory carrying costs and minimizing stockouts.

   o   Reduced Recall Costs: Improved quality control reduces the risk of product recalls, saving costs associated with recalls and regulatory penalties.

2. **Efficiency Gains:**

   o   Improved Productivity: Enhanced OEE (Overall Equipment Effectiveness) and reduced downtime increase production volumes and efficiency. For example, improving OEE from 37% to 70% can enhance annual returns by $15M to $21M for a typical factory.

   o   Streamlined Processes: Digitalization simplifies workflows, reducing cycle times and improving asset utilization.

3. **Revenue Growth Opportunities:**

   o   Faster Time-to-Market: Accelerated drug development and approval processes enable faster market entry for new products, increasing revenue potential.

   o   Personalized Medicine: Enables the development of personalized treatments, enhancing patient outcomes and creating new revenue streams.

4. **Increased Profitability:**

   o   Competitive Advantage: Pharma 4.0 Emerging technologies enhance competitiveness by improving operational efficiency and reducing operational costs, leading to increased product profitability.

   o   Regulatory Compliance: Simplifies compliance processes, reducing regulatory risks and associated costs.

By leveraging these financial benefits, pharmaceutical companies can enhance their profitability, drive business success, and improve patient outcomes.

Key Considerations

- Data Quality Management: Ensuring high-quality data is crucial for accurate insights and informed decision-making.

- Technological Integration: Leveraging advanced technologies like AI and IoT to analyse complex datasets.

- Regulatory Frameworks: Understanding and adhering to evolving regulatory standards to maintain compliance.

Challenges and Opportunities

- Challenges: Common challenges include managing cultural resistance, ensuring regulatory compliance, and integrating new technologies with existing systems.

- Opportunities: Offers opportunities for accelerated innovation, improved efficiency, and enhanced patient outcomes, ultimately driving business success and competitiveness in the pharmaceutical industry.

Cost Reduction Strategies: Automation, Predictive Maintenance, Reduced Inventory Costs

Here are some cost reduction strategies in Pharma 4.0, focusing on automation, predictive maintenance, and reduced inventory costs:

1. **Automation:**

   o Process Optimization: Automation streamlines manufacturing processes, reducing manual errors and improving plant efficiency. This leads to lower operational costs by minimizing waste and optimizing resource allocation.

   o Increased Productivity: Automated systems enhance productivity by allowing for continuous production with reduced downtime, resulting in higher output and lower costs per unit.

2. **Predictive Maintenance:**

   o Reduced Downtime: Predictive analytics help predict equipment failures, allowing for scheduled maintenance before unplanned downtime occurs. This reduces maintenance costs by up to 10% and decreases downtime.

   o Extended Equipment Life: Regular maintenance extends the life of equipment, reducing the need for premature replacements and associated costs.

3. **Reduced Inventory Costs:**

   o Just-in-Time Manufacturing: Pharma 4.0 enables just-in-time production, where companies produce only the required amount of inventory, reducing inventory holding costs and minimizing waste.

   o Predictive Analytics: Advanced analytics optimize inventory management by predicting demand more accurately, reducing stockouts and overstocking.

Assumptions

- Data Quality Management: Ensuring high-quality data is crucial for accurate insights and informed decision-making.

- Technological Integration: Leveraging advanced technologies like AI and IoT to analyse complex datasets.

- Regulatory Frameworks: Understanding and adhering to evolving regulatory standards to maintain compliance.

Think For

- Challenges: Common challenges include managing cultural resistance, ensuring regulatory compliance, and integrating new technologies with existing systems.

- Opportunities: Offers opportunities for accelerated innovation, improved efficiency, and enhanced patient outcomes, ultimately driving business success and competitiveness in the pharmaceutical industry.

Revenue growth opportunities: faster time-to-market, increased customer satisfaction

Pharma 4.0 offers significant revenue growth opportunities by enabling faster time-to-market for new drugs and increasing customer satisfaction through personalized and efficient experiences. Here's how these aspects drive revenue growth:

Faster Time-to-Market

1. Accelerated Drug Development:

   o Advanced Analytics and AI: Technologies like AI and machine learning streamline drug discovery by analysing vast chemical spaces, identifying lead compounds, and optimizing drug design. This reduces the time required for preclinical research and validation.

2. **Efficient Clinical Trials:**

   o Optimized Trial Design: AI-driven analytics improve patient recruitment and trial designs, reducing delays in clinical trials.

   o Real-Time Monitoring: IoT-enabled devices provide real-time data during trials, allowing for quicker adjustments to protocols and faster completion.

3. **Smart Manufacturing:**

   o Agile Production: Modular factories equipped with IoT sensors ensure flexible production processes, enabling rapid scaling of new drugs.

   o Reduced Lead Times: Automation minimizes downtime, ensuring quicker manufacturing cycles and faster delivery to market.

Increased Customer Satisfaction

1. **Personalized Medicine:**

   o Tailored Treatments: Pharma 4.0 technologies enable the collection and analysis of patient-specific data (e.g., genetic profiles, medical histories), allowing for the development of personalized therapies that improve treatment outcomes.

   o Targeted Therapies: AI helps identify patient subgroups most likely to benefit from specific treatments, enhancing efficacy and safety.

2. **Enhanced Patient Engagement:**

   o   Digital Health Platforms: Telemedicine services, wearable devices, and mobile apps empower patients to actively participate in their healthcare journey, improving adherence to treatment regimens and overall satisfaction.

   o   Proactive Monitoring: Continuous monitoring of patient health enables early detection of issues and timely interventions, fostering trust in pharmaceutical companies.

3. **Improved Customer Experiences:**

   o   CRM Integration: Platforms available in market consolidate customer data from multiple touchpoints, enabling personalized engagement strategies that increase loyalty.

   o   Omnichannel Support: Seamless support across channels ensures customers receive timely assistance, enhancing satisfaction.

By leveraging Pharma 4.0 technologies to reduce time-to-market and enhance customer satisfaction, pharmaceutical companies can unlock substantial revenue growth opportunities while improving patient outcomes.

Non-Financial Benefits of Pharma 4.0

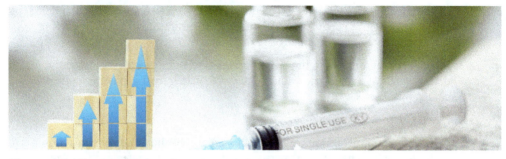

Pharma 4.0 offers several non-financial benefits that enhance the pharmaceutical industry's operations and outcomes. Here are some of these benefits:

1. **Enhanced Quality Control and Patient Safety:**

   o Real-Time Monitoring: Technologies like Cloud, IoT and AI enable real-time monitoring of manufacturing processes, ensuring early detection of quality issues and improving patient safety by reducing the risk of defective products.

   o Consistent Product Quality: Advanced analytics and machine learning ensure consistent product quality, reducing deviations and enhancing regulatory compliance.

2. **Improved Regulatory Compliance:**

   o Data Integrity: Pharma 4.0 technologies maintain data integrity through digital records and automated workflows, supporting regulatory compliance with standards like 21 CFR Part 11.

   o Simplified Audits: Digital solutions simplify audit processes by providing transparent and accessible data, reducing the likelihood of receiving FDA warning letters.

3. **Increased Agility and Flexibility:**

   o Modular Production Facilities: Modular facilities enabled by Pharma 4.0 allow for flexible production processes, enabling companies to respond quickly to changing market demands and customer needs.

   o Digital Twins: Digital twins simulate manufacturing processes, allowing for real-time analytics and optimization without disrupting actual production, enhancing operational flexibility.

4. **Workforce Benefits:**

   o Reduced Monotony: Automation reduces repetitive tasks, fostering innovative thinking and improving working conditions.

   o Performance Data Management: Digital tools enable better performance tracking and management, enhancing employee engagement and productivity.

5. Environmental Sustainability:

- o Waste Reduction: Lean manufacturing practices and predictive maintenance minimize waste, enhancing sustainability and reducing environmental impact.

- o Efficient Resource Use: Optimized processes ensure efficient use of resources, contributing to a more sustainable manufacturing environment.

By leveraging these non-financial benefits, pharmaceutical companies can enhance their operational efficiency, improve product quality, and maintain a competitive edge in the industry.

Key Considerations

- Data Quality Management: Ensuring high-quality data is crucial for accurate insights and informed decision-making.

- Technological Integration: Leveraging advanced technologies like AI and IoT to analyse complex datasets.

- Regulatory Frameworks: Understanding and adhering to evolving regulatory standards to maintain compliance.

Enhanced brand reputation, improved patient outcomes, increased employee engagement

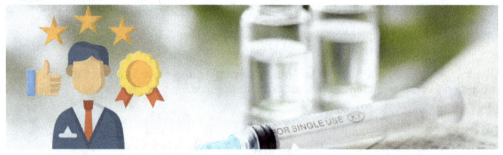

Here's how Pharma 4.0 enhances brand reputation, improves patient outcomes, and increases employee engagement:

Enhanced Brand Reputation

1. **Quality and Consistency:**

    o   Real-Time Monitoring: Pharma 4.0 emerging technologies ensure consistent product quality through real-time monitoring, reducing the risk of quality issues and enhancing brand reputation by maintaining high standards.

    o   Transparency and Compliance: Digital solutions provide transparent and reliable data management, supporting regulatory compliance and reinforcing trust in the brand.

2. **Innovation Leadership:**

    o   Adoption of Advanced Technologies: Companies that adopt Pharma 4.0 are seen as innovation leaders, enhancing their brand reputation by demonstrating a commitment to cutting-edge solutions.

Improved Patient Outcomes

1. **Personalized Medicine:**

    o   Tailored Treatments: Pharma 4.0 enables the development of personalized treatments by analyzing large-scale medical records and leveraging data insights to tailor therapies to individual patient needs.

    o   Targeted Therapies: AI helps identify patient subgroups that respond best to specific treatments, enhancing treatment efficacy and reducing adverse reactions.

2. **Faster Time-to-Market:**

    o   Accelerated Drug Development: Advanced analytics and machine learning accelerate drug discovery and development, enabling faster access to new treatments for patients.

Increased Employee Engagement

1. **Workforce Benefits:**

   o Reduced Monotony: Automation reduces repetitive tasks, fostering innovative thinking and improving working conditions.

   o Performance Data Management: Digital tools enable better performance tracking and management, enhancing employee engagement and productivity.

2. **Cultural Shift:**

   o Quality Culture: Pharma 4.0 fosters a culture of quality, collaboration, and continuous learning, empowering employees to take ownership of quality processes and make data-driven decisions.

   o Upskilling Opportunities: The adoption of advanced technologies provides opportunities for employees to develop new skills, enhancing job satisfaction and career advancement.

By leveraging these aspects, pharmaceutical companies can enhance their brand reputation, improve patient outcomes, and increase employee engagement, ultimately driving business success and competitiveness in the industry.

Sustainability and environmental benefits

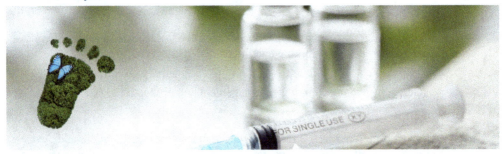

Pharma 4.0 offers several sustainability and environmental benefits by integrating advanced technologies into pharmaceutical manufacturing. Here are some key advantages:

1. Reduced Environmental Impact:

- o Energy Efficiency: Industry 4.0 technologies improve energy efficiency by optimizing resource utilization and reducing waste, which contributes to lowering greenhouse gas emissions and supporting net-zero policies.

- o Waste Minimization: Lean manufacturing principles and waste reduction strategies minimize the environmental footprint of pharmaceutical production.

2. Improved Resource Utilization:

- o Optimized Production Processes: Smart manufacturing solutions like automation and IoT enable more efficient use of resources, reducing the need for raw materials and minimizing waste generation.

- o Renewable Energy Integration: The use of renewable energy sources in manufacturing facilities further reduces the carbon footprint of the industry.

3. Enhanced Sustainability Reporting:

- o ESG Compliance: Pharma 4.0 technologies facilitate better tracking and reporting of environmental, social, and governance (ESG) metrics, ensuring transparency and accountability in sustainability efforts.

- o Data-Driven Insights: Advanced analytics provide insights that help identify areas for improvement in environmental sustainability, enabling proactive measures to reduce environmental impact.

4. Circular Economy Practices:

- o Recycling Programs: Implementing recycling programs for materials like packaging and laboratory consumables supports a circular economy, reducing waste and promoting sustainable practices.

By embracing these sustainability and environmental benefits, pharmaceutical companies can contribute to a greener future while enhancing operational efficiency and innovation.

Key Considerations

- Data Quality Management: Ensuring high-quality data is crucial for accurate insights and informed decision-making.

- Technological Integration: Leveraging advanced technologies like AI and IoT to analyse complex datasets.

- Regulatory Frameworks: Understanding and adhering to evolving regulatory standards to maintain compliance.

Challenges and Opportunities

- Challenges: Common challenges include managing cultural resistance, ensuring regulatory compliance, and integrating new technologies with existing systems.

- Opportunities: Offers opportunities for accelerated innovation, improved efficiency, and enhanced sustainability, ultimately driving business success and competitiveness in the pharmaceutical industry.

Implementing Pharma 4.0

Part IV: Implementing Pharma 4.0

Implementing Pharma 4.0 involves a strategic approach to integrating advanced digital technologies into pharmaceutical manufacturing. Here's a comprehensive guide to implementing Pharma 4.0:

Step-by-Step Implementation Guide

1. **Assess Current Capabilities:**

   o Inventory Existing Technologies: Evaluate current systems and technologies to identify areas for improvement and potential integration points for new technologies.

   o Gap Analysis: Conduct a gap analysis to determine what technologies and skills are needed to achieve Pharma 4.0 goals.

2. **Define Pharma 4.0 Vision:**

   o Strategic Alignment: Align Pharma 4.0 initiatives with overall business strategy and goals, ensuring that digital transformation supports core objectives.

   o Stakeholder Engagement: Engage stakeholders across departments to ensure a unified understanding of the vision and its benefits.

3. **Formulate a Digital Transformation Strategy:**

   o Roadmap Development: Create a detailed roadmap outlining key milestones, timelines, and resource allocation for the transformation process.

   o Change Management Plan: Develop a change management plan to address cultural and organizational changes required for successful implementation.

4. **Invest in Technologies:**

   o AI and IoT Integration: Implement AI, IoT, and other Industry 4.0 technologies to enhance manufacturing efficiency and quality control.

   o Cloud Computing: Leverage cloud platforms for scalable data management and collaboration.

5. **Enhance Workforce Skills:**

   o Training Programs: Provide comprehensive training programs to upskill employees in areas like AI, machine learning, and data analytics.

   o Talent Acquisition: Attract new talent with expertise in digital technologies to support transformation efforts.

6. **Data Management and Security:**

   o Data Governance: Establish robust data governance policies to ensure data quality, integrity, and security.

   o Cybersecurity Measures: Implement advanced cybersecurity measures to protect sensitive data and maintain compliance with regulatory standards.

7. **Monitor and Optimize:**

   o Continuous Monitoring: Implement real-time monitoring systems to track performance and identify areas for improvement.

   o Agile Methodologies: Adopt agile methodologies to quickly respond to changes and optimize processes based on feedback and data insights.

8. **Collaborate and Innovate:**

   o Partnerships and Collaborations: Foster partnerships with technology providers and other industry stakeholders to leverage best practices and accelerate innovation.

   o Innovation Culture: Encourage a culture of innovation within the organization, supporting experimentation and learning from failures.

Challenges in Implementation

- Regulatory Compliance: Ensuring that new technologies meet regulatory standards is a significant challenge. Regulatory frameworks often lag behind technological advancements, creating uncertainty for manufacturers.

- Data Privacy and Security: The use of Cloud, AI, IoT, and big data analytics generates vast amounts of sensitive data, requiring robust security measures to protect against cyber threats and ensure data integrity.

- Integration of Legacy Systems: Integrating new digital technologies with existing legacy systems can be complex and costly.

- Talent Acquisition and Retention: Pharma 4.0 requires specialized skills in areas like Cloud, AI, machine learning, and data analytics, which can be difficult to find and retain.

Strategic Planning for Pharma 4.0

Strategic planning for Pharma 4.0 involves a comprehensive approach to integrating advanced digital technologies into pharmaceutical manufacturing, enhancing operational efficiency, product quality, and innovation.

Here's a structured guide to strategic planning for Pharma 4.0:

1. **Establish Business-Driven Goals:**

   o Define Objectives: Align Pharma 4.0 initiatives with overall business strategy, focusing on operational excellence, product leadership, and customer intimacy.

   o Metrics of Success: Establish clear metrics to measure success, such as OEE improvements, quality enhancements, and time-to-market reductions.

2. **Implement a Comprehensive Strategy Design:**

   o Roadmap Development: Create a detailed roadmap outlining key milestones, timelines, and resource allocation for the transformation process.

   o Change Management Plan: Develop a change management plan to address cultural and organizational changes required for successful implementation.

3. **Leverage Data Analytics and Scenario Planning:**

   o Predictive Analytics: Use data analytics to predict market trends, patient needs, and potential disruptions, enabling proactive decision-making.

   o Scenario Planning: Conduct scenario planning to anticipate and prepare for future challenges and opportunities.

4. **Ensure Regulatory Compliance:**

   o Regulatory Alignment: Ensure that all digital transformation initiatives align with regulatory standards, such as GMP and GDP.

   o Compliance Roadmap: Develop a compliance roadmap to address evolving regulatory requirements.

5. Foster Innovation and Continuous Improvement:

- o Innovation Culture: Encourage a culture of innovation within the organization, supporting experimentation and learning from failures.

- o Continuous Improvement: Implement ongoing improvement processes using Lean and Six Sigma methodologies to optimize manufacturing operations.

Assumptions

- Data Quality Management: Ensuring high-quality data is crucial for accurate insights and informed decision-making.

- Technological Integration: Leveraging advanced technologies like AI and IoT to analyse complex datasets.

- Regulatory Frameworks: Understanding and adhering to evolving regulatory standards to maintain compliance.

Considerations

- Challenges: Common challenges include managing cultural resistance, ensuring regulatory compliance, and integrating new technologies with existing systems.

- Opportunities: Offers opportunities for accelerated innovation, improved efficiency, and enhanced patient outcomes, ultimately driving business success and competitiveness in the pharmaceutical industry.

By adopting these strategic planning principles, pharmaceutical companies can navigate the complexities of Pharma 4.0 and leverage its potential to drive innovation and efficiency.

Strategic Choices in Pharma 4.0

1. Product Leadership:

- o Innovation Focus: Pharma Companies focus on leveraging AI and ML to drive innovation in drug development.

- o Benefits: Enables the development of new treatments and personalized therapies.

2. Operational Excellence:

- o Efficiency Focus: Pharma Companies optimize manufacturing processes and digital supply chains to enhance efficiency and reduce costs.

- o Benefits: Improves product quality, reduces operational costs, and enhances regulatory compliance.

3. Customer Intimacy:

- o Patient-Centric Approach: Focuses on improving patient outcomes through personalized medicine and enhanced customer engagement.

- o Benefits: Enhances patient satisfaction and loyalty, driving long-term business success.

Each of these strategic focuses offers unique advantages and requires different competencies, allowing companies to tailor their approach based on their strengths and market position.

Steps for developing a strategic plan: assessing current state, setting objectives, creating a roadmap

Developing a strategic plan for Pharma 4.0 involves several key steps that help guide the transformation process. Here's a structured approach to creating a transformation strategic plan:

1. **Assess Current State:**

    o   Inventory Existing Technologies: Evaluate current systems and technologies to identify areas for improvement and potential integration points for new technologies.

    o   Gap Analysis: Conduct a gap analysis to determine what emerging technologies and skills are needed to achieve Pharma 4.0 goals.

    o   SWOT Analysis: Perform a SWOT analysis to understand strengths, weaknesses, opportunities, and threats related to the current state.

2. **Set Strategic Objectives:**

    o   Define Vision and Mission: Align Pharma 4.0 initiatives with the company's overall vision and mission, focusing on operational excellence, product leadership, and customer intimacy.

    o   Establish Key Performance Indicators (KPIs): Define clear metrics to measure success, such as OEE improvements, quality enhancements, and time-to-market reductions.

    o   Prioritize Objectives: Prioritize objectives based on business impact, feasibility, and resource availability.

3. **Create a Roadmap:**

    o   Short-Term and Long-Term Goals: Outline both short-term and long-term goals, ensuring alignment with overall business strategy.

    o   Milestones and Timelines: Establish specific milestones and timelines for each goal, including key deliverables and deadlines.

    o   Resource Allocation: Determine necessary resources (financial, human, technological) for each step of the roadmap.

4. **Develop a Change Management Plan:**

   o Cultural Transformation: Address cultural and organizational changes required for successful implementation, including technology and business processes training programs and communication strategies.

   o Stakeholder Engagement: Engage stakeholders across departments to ensure a unified understanding of the vision and its benefits.

5. **Monitor and Adjust:**

   o Continuous Monitoring: Implement real-time monitoring systems to track performance and identify areas for improvement.

   o Agile Methodologies: Adopt agile methodologies to quickly respond to changes and optimize processes based on feedback and data insights.

Key Considerations

- Data Quality Management: Ensuring high-quality data is crucial for accurate insights and informed decision-making.

- Technological Integration: Leveraging advanced technologies like AI and IoT to analyse complex datasets.

- Regulatory Frameworks: Understanding and adhering to evolving regulatory standards to maintain compliance.

Challenges and Opportunities

- Challenges: Common challenges include managing cultural resistance, ensuring regulatory compliance, and integrating new technologies with existing systems.

- Opportunities: Offers opportunities for accelerated innovation, improved efficiency, and enhanced patient outcomes, ultimately driving business success and competitiveness in the pharmaceutical industry.

By following these steps, pharmaceutical companies can develop a comprehensive strategic plan that aligns with their business goals and effectively guides their transition to Pharma 4.0.

Importance of stakeholder engagement and change management

Stakeholder engagement and change management are crucial components of successful digital transformation in the pharmaceutical industry, particularly in the context of Pharma 4.0. Here's why they are important:

1. **Building Trust and Transparency:**
   - Stakeholder Involvement: Engaging with diverse stakeholders, including patients, healthcare providers, regulators, and investors, helps build trust and enhances transparency. This is essential for maintaining a positive public image and ensuring accountability.
   - Improved Decision-Making: Stakeholder input provides valuable insights that can inform strategic decisions, ensuring that products meet real-world needs and regulatory requirements.

2. **Enhancing Patient Outcomes:**
   - Patient-Centric Approach: Engaging patients in drug development processes helps create treatments that better meet their needs, improving patient satisfaction and health outcomes.
   - Regulatory Compliance: Effective stakeholder engagement with regulators ensures compliance with evolving regulatory standards, reducing risks and enhancing product safety.

3. **Identifying Business Opportunities:**
   - Investor Engagement: Engaging with investors helps pharmaceutical companies understand their expectations and identify potential business opportunities, driving growth and innovation.

Importance of Change Management

1. **Smooth Transition:**
   - Organizational Change Management (OCM): Change management is vital for ensuring that employees adopt new processes and technologies, rather than reverting to traditional methods. This involves creating awareness, building desire for change, and establishing necessary knowledge and abilities.
   - Addressing Resistance: Planning for resistance and providing support during the change process helps mitigate potential disruptions and ensures successful implementation.

2. **Cultural Transformation:**

   o   Quality Culture: Implementing Pharma 4.0 requires a cultural shift towards a quality-centric organization. This involves fostering collaboration, innovation, and continuous learning, empowering employees to take ownership of quality processes.

   o   Leadership Commitment: Strong leadership is essential for championing digital innovation and providing resources for employees to adapt to new roles and technologies.

3. **Competitive Advantage:**

   o   Adaptability and Innovation: Effective change management enables pharmaceutical companies to adapt quickly to technological advancements and regulatory changes, maintaining competitiveness in a rapidly evolving industry.

By prioritizing stakeholder engagement and change management, pharmaceutical companies can ensure a successful transition to Pharma 4.0, enhancing operational efficiency, product quality, and innovation while maintaining regulatory compliance and stakeholder trust.

- Regulatory Frameworks: Understanding and adhering to evolving regulatory standards to maintain compliance.

Technological Integration

Technological integration is a critical aspect of Pharma 4.0, involving the seamless incorporation of advanced digital technologies into pharmaceutical manufacturing processes. Here's an overview of technological integration in Pharma 4.0:

1. **Key Technologies:**

   o Artificial Intelligence (AI) and Machine Learning (ML): Used for predictive analytics, process optimization, and personalized medicine development.

   o Internet of Things (IoT): Enables real-time monitoring and automation in manufacturing processes.

   o Big Data Analytics: Processes large datasets to extract insights that improve manufacturing efficiency and product quality.

   o Cloud Computing: Provides scalable data management and collaboration across different departments.

2. **Integration Challenges:**

   o Legacy System Integration: Integrating new technologies with existing legacy systems can be complex and costly.

   o Data Silos: Overcoming data silos and ensuring interoperability between different systems is crucial for seamless operations.

   o Cybersecurity Risks: Increased digitalization raises the risk of cyberattacks, which can compromise data integrity and business continuity.

3. **Benefits of Integration:**

   o Improved Efficiency: Enhances operational efficiency by automating manual processes and optimizing resource allocation.

   o Enhanced Quality Control: Real-time monitoring and predictive analytics ensure consistent product quality and early detection of deviations.

   o Innovation: Supports personalized medicine and accelerates innovation in drug development.

4. Implementation Strategies:

- o Holistic Approach: Develop a comprehensive strategy that addresses both technological and cultural aspects of change.
- o Stakeholder Engagement: Engage all stakeholders, including employees, suppliers, and regulatory bodies, to ensure alignment and support.
- o Continuous Monitoring: Implement real-time monitoring systems to track performance and identify areas for improvement.

By leveraging these technologies and strategies, pharmaceutical companies can enhance operational efficiency, improve product quality, and drive innovation while maintaining regulatory compliance.

Key Considerations

- Data Quality Management: Ensuring high-quality data is crucial for accurate insights and informed decision-making.
- Technological Integration: Leveraging advanced technologies like AI and IoT to analyse complex datasets.
- Regulatory Frameworks: Understanding and adhering to evolving regulatory standards to maintain compliance.

Challenges and Opportunities

- Challenges: Common challenges include managing cultural resistance, ensuring regulatory compliance, and integrating new technologies with existing systems.
- Opportunities: Offers opportunities for accelerated innovation, improved efficiency, and enhanced patient outcomes, ultimately driving business success and competitiveness in the pharmaceutical industry.

Overview of key technologies: AI, IoT, blockchain, cloud computing

Here's an overview of the key technologies driving Pharma 4.0, including AI, IoT, blockchain, and cloud computing:

Artificial Intelligence (AI):

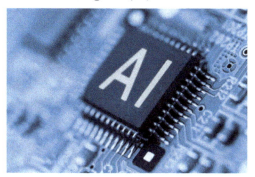

Applications: AI is used for accelerating drug development by analyzing large datasets, optimizing clinical trials, and developing personalized medicine. It predicts drug efficacy and toxicity, reducing the risk of failure in later stages.

Benefits: Enhances operational efficiency, accelerates innovation, and improves patient outcomes by tailoring treatments to individual needs

Internet of Things (IoT):

Applications: IoT devices enable real-time monitoring of manufacturing processes, ensuring quality control and optimizing production efficiency. They track products throughout the digital supply chain, enhancing transparency and traceability.

Benefits: Reduces downtime, improves product quality, and enhances digital supply chain management by providing real-time data insights.

Blockchain:

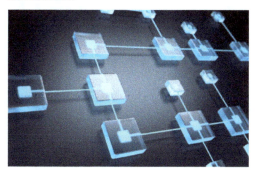

Applications: Blockchain technology ensures digital supply chain integrity by providing a tamper-proof system for tracking drugs from manufacturing to delivery. It enhances data security and transparency, reducing the risk of counterfeit drugs.

Benefits: Improves patient safety, optimizes logistics, and enhances regulatory compliance by maintaining immutable records.

Cloud Computing:

Applications: Cloud platforms facilitate scalable data storage and processing, enabling real-time collaboration and analysis across global teams. They support decentralized clinical trials and streamline drug development processes.

Benefits: Enhances operational efficiency, reduces costs, and accelerates innovation by providing secure and flexible data management solutions.

By integrating these technologies, pharmaceutical companies can transform their operations, enhance product quality, and improve patient outcomes while maintaining regulatory compliance.

Best practices for integrating new technologies with existing systems

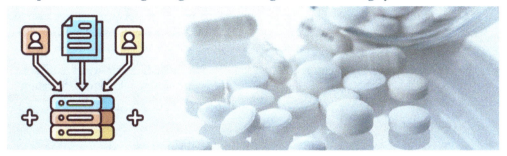

Integrating new technologies with existing systems in the pharmaceutical industry, particularly in the context of Pharma 4.0, requires a strategic approach to ensure seamless operations and maximize benefits. Here are some best practices for successful integration:

1. **Assessment and Planning:**

   o Evaluate Existing Systems: Conduct a thorough assessment of current systems to identify areas for improvement and potential integration points for new technologies.

   o Gap Analysis: Perform a gap analysis to determine what technologies and skills are needed to achieve Pharma 4.0 goals.

   o Strategic Alignment: Align new technologies with overall business strategy and goals, ensuring they support operational excellence, product leadership, and customer intimacy.

2. **Phased Integration Approach:**

   o Gradual Rollout: Implement new emerging technologies in phases, starting with pilot projects to test integration in a controlled environment. This approach minimizes disruptions to ongoing operations and allows for addressing any issues before full-scale implementation.

   o Feedback Loop: Use feedback from pilot projects to refine strategies and improve the integration process.

3. **Middleware Solutions:**

   o Interoperability: Use middleware to facilitate communication between legacy systems and new digital platforms, ensuring smooth data exchange and system interoperability.

   o API Integration: Leverage APIs to connect modern applications with older systems, enhancing data flow and functionality.

4. **Data Governance and Security:**

   o Data Integrity: Ensure data integrity by implementing robust data management systems that maintain data quality and security.

   o Cybersecurity Measures: Implement advanced cybersecurity measures to protect sensitive data and maintain compliance with regulatory standards.

5. **Change Management and Training:**

   o   Cultural Transformation: Foster a culture of innovation and change management to support the adoption of new technologies. This involves training employees and providing ongoing support to address resistance and enhance digital literacy.

   o   Stakeholder Engagement: Engage all stakeholders, including employees, suppliers, and regulatory bodies, to ensure alignment and support throughout the integration process.

6. **Partnerships and Collaborations:**

   o   Technology Providers: Collaborate with technology providers who specialize in Pharma 4.0 solutions to leverage their expertise and ensure compatibility with existing systems.

   o   Regulatory Bodies: Engage with regulatory bodies to address compliance challenges proactively and ensure that new technologies meet evolving regulatory standards.

By following these best practices, pharmaceutical companies can successfully integrate new technologies with existing systems, enhancing operational efficiency, product quality, and innovation while maintaining regulatory compliance.

Change Management and Training

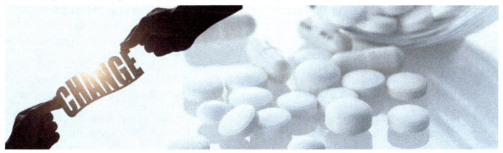

Change management and training are crucial components of successful digital transformation in the pharmaceutical industry, particularly in the context of Pharma 4.0. Here's an overview of how change management and training support the implementation of Pharma 4.0:

1. **Organizational Change Management (OCM):**

   o Structured Approach: OCM involves a structured approach to managing the people side of change, ensuring that employees adopt new processes and technologies effectively.

   o Awareness and Desire: Change management requires creating awareness about the need for technology and cultural change, building the desire to support it, and establishing the necessary knowledge and abilities for employees to perform in a new environment.

2. **Addressing Resistance:**

   o Cultural Transformation: Pharma 4.0 requires a significant cultural shift, as traditional processes and practices are deeply embedded in the industry's culture. Addressing resistance through structured OCM practices is crucial for achieving the desired outcomes of Pharma 4.0 projects.

   o Leadership Commitment: Strong leadership is essential for championing digital innovation and providing resources for employees to adapt to new roles and technologies.

Training in Pharma 4.0

1. **Employee Training and Development:**

   o Continuous Learning: A robust learning and development (L&D) strategy is necessary to help pharma employees adapt to an agile and ever-changing work environment. Employees must receive continuous training to develop industry-wide expertise and keep up with the fast-paced digital landscape.

   o Customized Training: Training should focus on general skills, sales, compliance, and role-specific competencies. It should be simple, mobile-friendly, and tailored to specific job roles to enhance adoption and effectiveness.

2. **Engaging Training Methods:**

- o   Video Training: Video training is becoming increasingly popular in Pharma 4.0 manufacturing, offering a more engaging and effective way to train employees. It allows for hands-on learning at the employee's own pace, improving retention and reducing costs.

- o   On-the-Job Training: Training applications can be configured to facilitate on-the-job training, allowing employees to learn while working without disrupting production.

By focusing on change management and training, pharmaceutical companies can ensure a smooth transition to Pharma 4.0, enhancing operational efficiency, product quality, and innovation while maintaining regulatory compliance.

Strategies for managing cultural and operational changes

Managing cultural and operational changes in the context of Pharma 4.0 requires a strategic approach that addresses both the people side of change and the technological aspects. Here are some strategies for managing these changes effectively:

Cultural Change Management

1. **Leadership Commitment:**
   - Visionary Leadership: Leaders must champion digital innovation, collaboration, and continuous improvement, providing necessary resources and support for employees to adapt to new technologies and roles.
   - Role Modelling: Leaders should model the behaviours and values they wish to see in the organization, demonstrating commitment to the change through their actions.

2. **Communication and Engagement:**
   - Transparent Communication: Clearly articulate the reasons behind the change, its benefits, and expected outcomes to all stakeholders. Encourage feedback and dialogue at all levels to minimize resistance.
   - Employee Involvement: Engage employees in the change process, allowing them to voice concerns and contribute ideas, fostering a sense of ownership and reducing resistance.

3. **Cultural Transformation:**
   - Quality Culture: Foster a culture of quality, collaboration, and continuous learning, empowering employees to take ownership of quality processes and make data-driven decisions.
   - People-Centric Approach: Prioritize employee well-being and involvement, ensuring that cultural shifts are supported by a strong organizational culture.

Operational Change Management

1. **Organizational Change Management (OCM):**

   o   Structured Approach: Implement a structured OCM process to manage the people side of change, ensuring that employees adopt new processes and technologies effectively.

   o   Awareness and Desire: Create awareness about the need for change, build the desire to support it, and establish necessary knowledge and abilities for employees to perform in a new environment.

2. **Change Control Process:**

   o   Risk Assessment: Conduct thorough risk assessments for each proposed change to identify potential impacts on product quality, safety, and regulatory compliance.

   o   Documentation and Validation: Maintain comprehensive documentation and perform testing and validation of changes before implementation to ensure they are well-controlled and do not introduce new risks.

3. **Digital Maturity Model:**

   o   Holistic Strategy: Adopt a holistic strategy that integrates digital technologies across all levels of the organization, ensuring alignment with business objectives and quality standards.

   o   Stages of Digital Maturity: Progress through stages of digital maturity, from initial adoption to optimized integration, ensuring that technology supports operational excellence and innovation.

By implementing these strategies, pharmaceutical companies can effectively manage cultural and operational changes, ensuring a successful transition to Pharma 4.0.

Training programs for enhancing digital literacy

Enhancing digital literacy is crucial for professionals in the pharmaceutical industry, particularly as it transitions towards Pharma 4.0.

Here are some strategies and examples for training programs aimed at improving digital literacy:

1. **Curriculum Development:**

   o Incorporating Digital Literacy: Integrate digital literacy into initial education and training standards for pharmacists and technicians. This includes theoretical understanding of health informatics, familiarity with diverse digital technologies, and applied informatics in patient-centric care and interprofessional collaboration.

   o Continuous Updates: Regularly update curricula to align with emerging digital technologies and practices, ensuring that professionals remain adept in using the latest tools and systems.

2. **Training Formats:**

   o Blended Learning: Use blended pedagogical strategies combining traditional teaching methods with online learning platforms. This approach allows for flexible learning and can include team-based learning, problem-solving activities, and immediate feedback.

   o Online Courses: Offer online training modules covering topics like electronic health records (EHRs), telemedicine, and clinical decision support systems (CDSSs). These courses can significantly improve knowledge, attitudes, and confidence in health informatics.

3. **Practical Application:**

   o Case Studies and Projects: Incorporate practical examples and case studies that demonstrate the use of digital technologies in real-world scenarios. This helps learners understand how to apply digital skills in patient care and service delivery.

   o Data Science Training: Provide training in data analysis to enhance service delivery, emphasizing data privacy, patient consent, and legal requirements.

4. Professional Development:

- o Continuous Professional Development (CPD): Offer CPD activities that focus on digital leadership, change management, stakeholder engagement, and risk management in digital projects. These modules should be tailored to different career stages and roles within pharmacy.

- o Workshops and Certifications: Provide workshops and certifications in areas such as data analytics, automation, and regulatory compliance to upskill employees and keep them current with industry trends.

Future Directions & Trends

Part V: Future Directions & Trends

Future Directions in Pharma 4.0

Here's an overview of future directions in Pharma 4.0, highlighting emerging trends and strategic priorities:

1. **Advancements In AI and Machine Learning:**

   o Predictive Analytics: AI will continue to play a crucial role in predictive analytics, enhancing drug discovery and optimizing clinical trials.

   o Personalized Medicine: AI-driven personalized medicine will become more prevalent, tailoring treatments to individual patient needs.

2. **Integration of Emerging Technologies:**

   o Blockchain and IoT: Technologies like blockchain and IoT will further enhance supply chain transparency and product authenticity, ensuring patient safety and regulatory compliance.

   o Digital Twins: The use of digital twins will become more widespread, allowing for real-time simulation and optimization of manufacturing processes.

3. **Data-Driven Decision Making:**

   o Big Data Analytics: The pharmaceutical industry will increasingly rely on big data analytics to extract insights that improve manufacturing efficiency, product quality, and patient outcomes.

   o Data Governance: Robust data governance will be essential to ensure data integrity and security.

4. **Sustainability and Supply Chain Resilience:**

   o Smart Manufacturing: Companies will focus on smart manufacturing to enhance supply chain efficiency and sustainability, reducing environmental impact while maintaining operational efficiency.

   o Global Supply Chain Optimization: The use of Cloud, AI and digital tools will optimize supply chains, enhancing resilience against geopolitical uncertainties and ensuring consistent product delivery.

5. **Regulatory Evolution:**

o Evolving Regulatory Frameworks: Regulatory bodies will continue to adapt to technological advancements, ensuring compliance while fostering innovation.

o Collaboration with Regulators: Pharmaceutical companies will need to collaborate closely with regulatory bodies to address compliance challenges proactively.

By embracing these future directions, pharmaceutical companies can drive innovation, enhance operational efficiency, and improve patient outcomes while maintaining regulatory compliance.

Future Trends in Pharma 4.0

Here are some future trends in Pharma 4.0, highlighting how advanced technologies will continue to transform the pharmaceutical industry:

1. **Advanced AI and Machine Learning:**

   o Predictive Analytics: AI will continue to play a crucial role in predictive analytics, enhancing drug discovery and optimizing clinical trials by analysing large datasets to predict drug efficacy and toxicity.

   o Personalized Medicine: AI-driven personalized medicine will become more prevalent, tailoring treatments to individual patient needs based on genetic profiles and medical histories.

2. **Integration of Emerging Technologies:**

   o Blockchain and IoT: Technologies like blockchain and IoT will further enhance supply chain transparency and product authenticity, ensuring patient safety and regulatory compliance. Blockchain will provide immutable records, while IoT will enable real-time monitoring of products throughout the supply chain.

   o Digital Twins: The use of digital twins will become more widespread, allowing for real-time simulation and optimization of manufacturing processes without disrupting actual production.

3. **Data-Driven Decision Making:**

   o Big Data Analytics: The pharmaceutical industry will increasingly rely on big data analytics to extract insights that improve manufacturing efficiency, product quality, and patient outcomes.

   o Data Governance: Robust data governance will be essential to ensure data integrity and security, supporting compliance with evolving regulatory standards.

4. **Sustainability and Supply Chain Resilience:**

   o Smart Manufacturing: Companies will focus on smart manufacturing to enhance supply chain efficiency and sustainability, reducing environmental impact while maintaining operational efficiency.

   o Global Supply Chain Optimization: The use of AI and digital tools will optimize supply chains, enhancing resilience against geopolitical uncertainties and ensuring consistent product delivery.

5. **Regulatory Evolution:**

   o Evolving Regulatory Frameworks: Regulatory bodies will continue to adapt to technological advancements, ensuring compliance while fostering innovation.

   o Collaboration with Regulators: Pharmaceutical companies will need to collaborate closely with regulatory bodies to address compliance challenges proactively.

By embracing these future trends, pharmaceutical companies can drive innovation, enhance operational efficiency, and improve patient outcomes while maintaining regulatory compliance.

Emerging technologies & innovations: GenAI, Digital Twins, Smart Manufacturing.

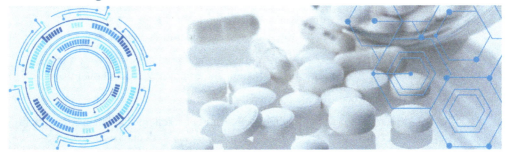

Here's an overview of emerging technologies and innovations in Pharma 4.0, focusing on Generative AI (GenAI), digital twins, and smart manufacturing:

Generative AI (GenAI)

1. **Applications in Drug Development:**
   - Molecule Generation: GenAI can generate new molecules with specific properties, accelerating drug development by reducing the time and cost associated with traditional screening methods.
   - Lead Optimization: GenAI helps optimize lead compounds by generating variants with improved pharmacological properties, enhancing efficacy and safety.

2. **Personalized Medicine:**
   - Tailored Treatments: GenAI can design personalized drugs optimized for specific patient populations, improving treatment outcomes and reducing side effects.

3. **Clinical Trials Optimization:**
   - Patient Stratification: GenAI identifies patient subgroups likely to respond to treatments, streamlining clinical trials and accelerating drug development.

Digital Twins

1. **Process Simulation:**
   - Real-Time Monitoring: Digital twins simulate manufacturing processes in real-time, allowing for predictive maintenance and optimization without disrupting production.
   - Quality Control: They help predict quality batches and manage waste, ensuring consistent product quality.

2. **Patient Digital Twins:**
   - Personalized Treatments: Digital twins can simulate patient responses to treatments, aiding in the development of personalized therapies.

Smart Manufacturing

1. **Automation and Efficiency:**

   o IoT and Robotics: Smart manufacturing integrates IoT sensors and robotics to automate processes, reduce errors, and enhance operational efficiency.

   o Predictive Maintenance: Real-time monitoring and predictive analytics minimize downtime, ensuring continuous production and improving product quality.

2. **Supply Chain Optimization:**

   o Real-Time Tracking: Technologies like IoT and blockchain enable real-time tracking of products, enhancing supply chain transparency and reducing risks.

3. **Regulatory Compliance:**

   o Digital Records: Smart manufacturing supports regulatory compliance by maintaining accurate digital records and ensuring data integrity.

By leveraging these emerging technologies, pharmaceutical companies can enhance operational efficiency, improve product quality, and drive innovation in drug development and manufacturing.

Future challenges and opportunities

Here's an overview of future challenges and opportunities in the pharmaceutical industry, particularly in the context of Pharma 4.0:

Future Challenges

1. **Regulatory Complexities:**

   o Evolving Regulations: Regulatory bodies are continuously updating standards to keep pace with technological advancements, requiring pharmaceutical companies to adapt quickly to maintain compliance.

   o Global Variability: Different regulatory requirements across countries complicate compliance efforts, necessitating a deep understanding of regional regulations.

2. **Talent Shortages:**

   o Specialized Skills: The demand for specialized talent in AI, biotechnology, and personalized medicine outpaces supply, making it difficult to attract and retain skilled professionals.

   o Workforce Evolution: The industry must evolve its workforce to meet the needs of emerging technologies, requiring significant investment in training and development.

3. **Supply Chain Disruptions:**

   o Global Uncertainties: Digital Supply chains face disruptions due to geopolitical uncertainties, natural disasters, and manufacturing constraints, emphasizing the need for real-time tracking and predictive analytics.

   o Resilience Strategies: Companies must adopt strategies to build resilient supply chains, leveraging digital tools to mitigate risks and ensure continuity.

4. **Environmental and Sustainability Concerns:**

   o Green Manufacturing: There is growing pressure to adopt sustainable practices, reducing carbon footprints and environmental impact through green chemistry and circular economy principles.

   o Regulatory Expectations: Regulatory bodies increasingly expect companies to prioritize sustainability, making it a critical aspect of operational strategy.

Future Opportunities

1. **Digital Transformation and AI:**

   o Accelerated Innovation: AI and machine learning will continue to accelerate drug discovery, optimize clinical trials, and enhance personalized medicine, driving innovation and efficiency.

   o Data-Driven Insights: Big data analytics will provide valuable insights to improve manufacturing processes, product quality, and patient outcomes.

2. **Personalized Medicine:**

   o Tailored Treatments: Advances in genomics and biotechnology will propel personalized medicine into the mainstream, improving treatment efficacy and patient satisfaction.

   o Precision Therapies: The development of precision therapies will become more prevalent, leveraging AI to identify patient subgroups that respond best to specific treatments.

3. **Sustainability and Green Manufacturing:**

   o Environmental Benefits: Companies adopting sustainable practices will not only reduce their environmental impact but also enhance their brand reputation and compliance with evolving regulatory standards.

   o Cost Savings: Sustainable manufacturing can lead to cost savings through efficient resource use and reduced waste.

4. **Global Market Expansion:**

   o Emerging Markets: The growth of emerging markets like US,EU, India and China presents opportunities for pharmaceutical companies to expand their global footprint and capitalize on cost efficiencies.

   o Innovation Hubs: Establishing innovation hubs in these regions can foster collaboration and accelerate the development of new treatments.

By addressing these challenges and leveraging these opportunities, pharmaceutical companies can navigate the future landscape effectively, driving innovation and growth while maintaining regulatory compliance.

Conclusion and Recommendations

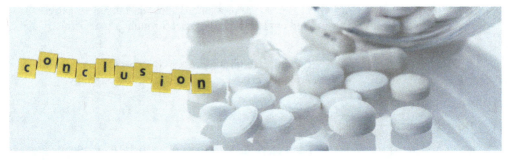

Conclusion

Pharma 4.0 represents a transformative shift in the pharmaceutical industry, leveraging advanced technologies like Cloud, AI, IoT, and blockchain to enhance operational efficiency, product quality, and innovation. By integrating these technologies, companies can accelerate drug discovery, optimize manufacturing processes, and improve patient outcomes. However, successful implementation requires careful planning, stakeholder engagement, and a focus on regulatory compliance.

Recommendations

1. **Strategic Planning:**

   o   Align with Business Strategy: Ensure that Pharma 4.0 initiatives align with overall business goals, focusing on operational excellence, product leadership, and customer intimacy.

   o   Roadmap Development: Create a detailed roadmap outlining key milestones, timelines, and resource allocation for the transformation process.

2. **Technological Integration:**

   o   Holistic Approach: Adopt a holistic strategy that integrates digital technologies across all levels of the organization, ensuring alignment with business objectives and quality standards.

   o   Legacy System Integration: Prioritize integrating new technologies with existing legacy systems to minimize disruptions and enhance operational efficiency.

3. **Change Management and Training:**

   o   Cultural Transformation: Foster a culture of innovation and change management to support the adoption of new technologies. This involves training employees and providing ongoing support to address resistance and enhance digital literacy.

   o   Continuous Learning: Implement continuous learning programs to upskill employees in areas like AI, machine learning, and data analytics.

4. **Regulatory Compliance:**

   o   Regulatory Alignment: Ensure that all digital transformation initiatives align with regulatory standards, such as GMP and Annex 1.

   o   Collaboration with Regulators: Engage with regulatory bodies to address compliance challenges proactively and ensure that new technologies meet evolving regulatory requirements.

5. **Stakeholder Engagement:**

   o   Patient-Centric Approach: Engage patients in drug development processes to create treatments that better meet their needs, improving patient satisfaction and health outcomes.

   o   Supply Chain Partnerships: Foster partnerships with suppliers and distributors to enhance supply chain transparency and resilience.

By following these recommendations, pharmaceutical companies can successfully navigate the transition to Pharma 4.0, enhancing their competitiveness and driving business success while improving patient outcomes.

Summary of key points and takeaways

Here's a summary of key points and takeaways related to Pharma 4.0:

Summary of Key Points

1. **Pharma 4.0 Overview:**

   o   Digital Transformation: Pharma 4.0 involves the integration of advanced digital technologies like Cloud, AI, IoT, and blockchain to transform pharmaceutical manufacturing and drug development.

   o   Benefits: Enhances operational efficiency, improves product quality, accelerates innovation, and enhances patient outcomes.

2. **Key Technologies:**

   o   AI and Machine Learning: Accelerate drug development, optimize clinical trials, and enable personalized medicine.

   o   IoT and Blockchain: Enhance supply chain transparency, ensure product authenticity, and improve manufacturing efficiency.

   o   Cloud Computing: Facilitates scalable data management and collaboration across global teams.

3. **Operational Efficiency and Productivity:**

   o   Real-Time Monitoring: IoT devices enable real-time monitoring of manufacturing processes, reducing downtime and enhancing efficiency.

   o   Predictive Maintenance: Predictive analytics minimize unplanned downtime, ensuring continuous production.

4. **Quality and Compliance:**

   o   Enhanced Quality Control: Real-time monitoring and automation ensure consistent product quality and early detection of deviations.

   o   Regulatory Compliance: Digital solutions simplify compliance processes through automation and data integrity.

5. **Innovation and Competitiveness:**

   o   Accelerated Drug Development: AI and data analytics accelerate drug discovery and approval processes.

   o   Personalized Medicine: Enables the development of tailored treatments, enhancing patient outcomes and creating new revenue streams.

6. **Financial Benefits:**

   o   Cost Savings: Automation and process optimization reduce operational costs.

   o   Revenue Growth: Faster time-to-market and personalized treatments increase revenue potential.

7. **Non-Financial Benefits:**

   o Enhanced Brand Reputation: Improved quality and compliance enhance brand reputation.

   o Increased Employee Engagement: Training and upskilling opportunities improve employee satisfaction.

8. **Implementation Strategies:**

   o Strategic Planning: Align Pharma 4.0 initiatives with business strategy.

   o Change Management: Foster a culture of innovation and provide ongoing training.

   o Regulatory Compliance: Collaborate with regulators to address compliance challenges.

Key Takeaways

- Embrace Digital Transformation· Leverage advanced technologies to drive innovation and efficiency.

- Focus on Quality and Compliance: Ensure that digital solutions enhance product quality and simplify regulatory compliance.

- Invest in Employee Development: Provide training to enhance digital literacy and support cultural transformation.

- Collaborate with Stakeholders: Engage with patients, suppliers, and regulators to maximize benefits and address challenges.

By understanding and implementing these key points, pharmaceutical companies can successfully transition to Pharma 4.0, driving business success and improving patient outcomes.

Recommendations for pharmaceutical companies embarking on Pharma 4.0 journeys

Here are some recommendations for pharmaceutical companies embarking on a Pharma 4.0 journey:

1. **Strategic Planning:**
   - Align with Business Strategy: Ensure that Pharma 4.0 initiatives align with overall business goals, focusing on operational excellence, product leadership, and customer intimacy.
   - Roadmap Development: Create a detailed roadmap outlining key milestones, timelines, and resource allocation for the transformation process.

2. **Technological Integration:**
   - Holistic Approach: Adopt a holistic strategy that integrates digital technologies across all levels of the organization, ensuring alignment with business objectives and quality standards.
   - Legacy System Integration: Prioritize integrating new technologies with existing legacy systems to minimize disruptions and enhance operational efficiency.

3. **Change Management and Training:**
   - Cultural Transformation: Foster a culture of innovation and change management to support the adoption of new technologies. This involves training employees and providing ongoing support to address resistance and enhance digital literacy.
   - Continuous Learning: Implement continuous learning programs to upskill employees in areas like AI, machine learning, and data analytics.

4. **Regulatory Compliance:**
   - Regulatory Alignment: Ensure that all digital transformation initiatives align with regulatory standards, such as GMP and Annex 1.
   - Collaboration with Regulators: Engage with regulatory bodies to address compliance challenges proactively and ensure that new technologies meet evolving regulatory requirements.

5. **Stakeholder Engagement:**
   - Patient-Centric Approach: Engage patients in drug development processes to create treatments that better meet their needs, improving patient satisfaction and health outcomes.
   - Supply Chain Partnerships: Foster partnerships with suppliers and distributors to enhance supply chain transparency and resilience.

6. **Data Governance:**

   o Data Quality Management: Ensure high-quality data is crucial for accurate insights and informed decision-making.

   o Data Security: Implement robust cybersecurity measures to protect sensitive data and maintain compliance with regulatory standards.

7. **Innovation and Agility:**

   o Adopt Agile Methodologies: Implement agile methodologies to quickly respond to changes and optimize processes based on feedback and data insights.

   o Encourage Innovation: Foster a culture of innovation within the organization, supporting experimentation and learning from failures.

By following these recommendations, pharmaceutical companies can successfully navigate the transition to Pharma 4.0, enhancing their competitiveness and driving business success while improving patient outcomes.

Appendices

Appendices

Glossary of Terms

1. **Artificial Intelligence (AI):**
    - Definition: AI refers to the development of computer systems that can perform tasks that typically require human intelligence, such as learning, problem-solving, and decision-making.
    - Applications in Pharma 4.0: AI is used for predictive analytics, process optimization, and personalized medicine development.

2. **Internet of Things (IoT):**
    - Definition: IoT involves a network of physical devices, vehicles, home appliances, and other items embedded with sensors, software, and connectivity, allowing them to collect and exchange data.
    - Applications in Pharma 4.0: IoT enables real-time monitoring and automation in manufacturing processes, enhancing operational efficiency and product quality.

3. **Big Data Analytics:**
    - Definition: Big data analytics involves the process of examining large data sets to uncover hidden patterns, correlations, market trends, and customer preferences.
    - Applications in Pharma 4.0: Big data analytics processes large datasets to extract insights that improve manufacturing efficiency and product quality.

4. **Cloud Computing:**
    - Definition: Cloud computing is a model for delivering computing services over the internet, providing on-demand access to a shared pool of configurable computing resources.
    - Applications in Pharma 4.0: Cloud computing provides scalable data management and collaboration across different departments.

5. **Blockchain:**
    - Definition: Blockchain is a decentralized, distributed ledger technology that records transactions across many computers so that any involved record cannot be altered retroactively.
    - Applications in Pharma 4.0: Blockchain enhances supply chain transparency and ensures product authenticity.

6. **Digital Twins:**
    - Definition: A digital twin is a virtual replica of a physical entity or system, used for real-time monitoring and simulation.
    - Applications in Pharma 4.0: Digital twins simulate manufacturing processes, allowing for real-time analytics and optimization without disrupting actual production.

7. **Generative AI (GenAI):**

   o Definition: GenAI refers to AI systems capable of generating new content, such as text, images, or molecules, based on patterns learned from existing data.

   o Applications in Pharma 4.0: GenAI accelerates drug discovery by generating new molecules with specific properties.

8. **Smart Manufacturing:**

   o Definition: Smart manufacturing involves the integration of advanced technologies like Cloud, AI, IoT, and robotics to enhance manufacturing efficiency and flexibility.

   o Applications in Pharma 4.0: Smart manufacturing optimizes production processes, reduces waste, and improves product quality.

ROI Calculator Template

Section 1: Initial Investment

1. Hardware and Software Expenses:

   o Cost of purchasing and implementing new technologies like Cloud, AI, IoT, and cloud computing.

2. Training and Integration Costs:

   o Expenses related to training employees and integrating new systems with existing infrastructure.

3. Consulting and Advisory Fees:

   o Costs associated with hiring consultants for strategy development and implementation guidance.

4. Total Initial Investment:

   o Sum of all initial costs.

Section 2: Annual Operating Costs

1. Maintenance and Support:

   o Ongoing costs for maintaining and supporting new technologies.

2. Training and Upgrades:

   o Continuous training and upgrade costs to ensure employees remain proficient with evolving technologies.

3. Energy and Resource Costs:

   o Any additional energy or resource costs associated with new technologies.

4. Total Annual Operating Costs:

   o Sum of all annual costs.

Section 3: Expected Benefits

1. Cost Savings:

   o Reductions in operational costs through automation and process optimization.

2. Revenue Growth:

   o Increases in revenue due to faster time-to-market for new products and improved customer satisfaction.

3. Productivity Improvements:

   o Enhanced efficiency and productivity leading to increased output or reduced labour costs.

4. Total Expected Benefits:

   o Sum of all expected benefits.

Section 4: ROI Calculation

1. Time Frame:

   o   Duration of the project in years.

2. Total Costs:

   o   Initial investment + (Annual operating costs × Time frame).

3. Total Benefits:

   o   Expected benefits × Time frame.

4. ROI Calculation:

   o   ROI = (Total Benefits - Total Costs) / Total Costs * 100%.

Example of Use

Indicating data, just as a sample to explain process of calculation

Let's assume a pharmaceutical company invests $1 million in AI and IoT technologies to enhance manufacturing efficiency. The annual operating costs are $200,000, and the project duration is 5 years. The company expects to save $300,000 annually in operational costs and increase revenue by $500,000 per year due to faster time-to-market.

- Total Initial Investment: $1,000,000

- Total Annual Operating Costs: $200,000

- Total Costs: $1,000,000 + ($200,000 × 5) = $2,000,000

- Total Expected Benefits: ($300,000 + $500,000) × 5 = $4,000,000

- ROI: ($4,000,000 - $2,000,000) / $2,000,000 * 100% = 100%

Additional Resources

Here's a list of recommended books, articles, and websites for further learning on Pharma 4.0 and digital transformation in the pharmaceutical industry:

Books

1. "Pharmaceutical industry 4.0: Future, Challenges & Application":

   o This book provides insights into key technologies modernizing pharmaceutical manufacturing and facilitating digital transformation.

2. "Digital Transformation and Regulatory Considerations for Biopharmaceutical and Healthcare Manufacturers, Volume 2":

   o Offers detailed information on digital transformation in the biopharmaceutical sector, focusing on data analytics and regulatory compliance.

Articles

1. "Validating Pharma 4.0 for Smart Manufacturing":

   o Discusses the validation process for Pharma 4.0 technologies in smart manufacturing environments.

2. "Pharma 4.0: Accelerating Digital Transformation in the Pharmaceutical Industry":

   o Explores how Pharma 4.0 leverages emerging technologies to optimize processes and improve patient outcomes.

Websites

1. ISPE Pharma 4.0 Resources:

   o Provides practical guidance and operating models for implementing Pharma 4.0, focusing on regulatory compliance and digital transformation.

2. What fix Blog on Pharma Digital Transformation:

   o Offers insights into digital transformation trends, challenges, and examples in the pharmaceutical industry.

3. IPI Academy Courses:

   o Offers training sessions on Pharma 4.0, focusing on smart technologies and digital transformation strategies.

About the Author

About the Author

Dr Jayant Joshi, has Engineering and Management background with more than 45 years of experience. His passion is **Adoption of Technologies to achieve Operational and Business Excellence**.

During his long career, he has designed, developed and implemented Management and Technology Enterprise solutions with Large and Mid- size companies from Strategy to Audit / Validation to Achieve remarkable performance improvements.

He operates a **YouTube channel** named **CENTER OF EXCELLENCE PHARMA 4.0.** This channel has more than 300 videos focused on Emerging Technologies, Digital Transformation and Pharma 4.0. These videos have depth from Strategy, Roadmap, Implementation, Change Management to Audits and Validations. Users can access it through the following link: https://www.youtube.com/@COE-PHARMA4.0

Additionally, Dr. Jayant Joshi offers a **comprehensive course on Udemy** called **SMART MANUFACTURING IN PHARMA**. This course provides an in-depth exploration of Smart Manufacturing principles and technologies applied in the pharmaceutical sector, covering digitalization, automation, and data-driven decision-making to enhance efficiency, quality, and compliance. Participants can find the course at: https://www.udemy.com/course/smart-manufacturing-in-pharma/

Dr. Jayant Joshi also runs a **Podcast** titled **Center of Excellence - Pharma 4.**0 which explores Smart Manufacturing principles and technologies within the pharmaceutical sector. The podcast covers how digitalization, automation, and data-driven decision-making are enhancing efficiency, quality, and compliance in pharmaceutical manufacturing processes. It caters to professionals in pharmaceuticals, technology, and those interested in the future of healthcare or pharmaceutical manufacturing. Access the podcast here: https://pharma4coe.podbean.com

He can be reached at

https://www.linkedin.com/in/jayantjoshi/

https://respa.com

https://www.facebook.com/jayant.joshi.1422

https://x.com/jayantbjoshi